With God's

The Great Guru Nanak
Volume 2

The Great Guru Nanak
Volume 2

Authored by,
Gurdeyal Singh

Translated by,
Harjinder Singh

www.akaalpublishers.com

First Published by Akaal Publishers in 2020

ISBN 978-1-9996052-3-0

Cover Design by Jag Lall

www.akaalpublishers.com

Dedicated to the first Sikh,
Bebe Nanaki Jee

May we all enshrine her faith

Preface

I would like to begin by apologising to readers for the time taken to publish Volume 2 which you are reading now. Volume 1 of this book has been in circulation for many years and many editions have been published.

I have added a glossary of terms at the end of this book to assist readers with terms in Gurmukhi. Much like the other books I have written or translated, I have broken rules of English grammar when referring to Guru Jee by using plural terms, not singular ones; this is the tradition in the Sikh faith when addressing the elevated.

Bhai Gurdeyal Singh Jee did an excellent job writing the original book which makes up a set of books called 'Dharam Pothis', published by Damdami Taksal in Punjabi. This book includes a complete translation of Dharam Pothi 2 and some chapters from Dharam Pothi 3.

Any errors in translation or grammar are solely mine and I will endeavour to correct any errors that readers may find.

A big thank you to Jajhar Singh and Rajveer Kaur for excellent feedback on proofing the final book. Thanks to Harmanjit Kaur, Manvir Kaur and Varinder Kaur for helping with the administrative tasks in collating this book.

Thank you to Jag Lall for the cover design.

I hope you enjoy the book and I look forward to readers' feedback.

Harjinder Singh
November 2020

Contents

Chapter 1
Sri Guru Nanak Dev Jee and Bhai Lalo

After leaving the work of the store (modhikhana), Sri Guru Nanak Dev Jee left Sultanpur with Bhai Mardana to start preaching the path of truthful living.

Bhai Mardana asked, "Guru Jee, where shall you go?"

Guru Jee replied, "Eminabad - to the house of the carpenter (tarkhan), Lalo."

Those of high castes used to refer to Bhai Lalo as lowly and a Shooder (low caste). They would stay away from him in order to avoid cross-contamination from him (as that was the level of caste-based discrimination). Bhai Lalo earned an honest living which he lived off: he served guests, did their Seva (voluntary devotional service), was devoted to God and he did Bhagti (lived a life full of devotional prayer and practice).

Guru Jee was from a higher caste and was a Khatri (warrior caste), from the Bedi ancestry. Guru Jee had no pride of their caste. Guru Jee saw those as devoted to God as superior beings and did not discriminate against them based on caste, nor did Guru Jee believe in issues of pollution/cross-contamination of associating with them.

It took Guru Jee 17 days to travel to Bhai Lalo's house in Eminabad. Eminabad is today in District Gujranwala in Pakistan. When Guru Jee arrived, Bhai Lalo stood up out of respect and bowed respectfully at their feet. Having their blessed sight (Darshan), he attained much peace.

Guru Jee said to Bhai Lalo, "May God remain in your thoughts. Sit and conduct your work."

Bhai Lalo asked, "Where have you come from? Where is your home and tell me your name?"

Guru Jee said, "Our home is very far from here. We are foreigners. You will come to know of our name yourself."

Bhai Lalo said, "I have heard that a great spiritualist called Nanak has been revealed to the world. Are you that Nanak? Without your confirmation, I cannot believe this."

Bhai Mardana said, "My name is Mardana. I am the Marasi (low caste minstrel) of the Bedi family. Sri Guru Nanak Dev Jee is my master. I travel with them."

Hearing this, Bhai Lalo clasped his hands and bowed at the feet of Guru Jee. He put out a cot (Manja) for Guru Jee to be seated upon. Guru Jee sat down.

After getting permission off Guru Jee, Bhai Lalo left the room to prepare food. Bhai Mardana asked Guru Jee, "Who is this man? He seems to have great fortune (in that Guru Jee has come to his home)."

Guru Jee replied, "Know him to be saintly. He has spent many lives doing Bhagti."

After some time, Bhai Lalo came and said, "Please come and eat food."

Guru Jee said, "Bring it here."

Hearing this, Bhai Lalo brought a tray of food out: in it was chapatti made with Baajra (pearl millet flour) and 'sarao da saag' (mustard grains) to compliment the chapatti (this dish is a staple of the poor and seen to be simple food). Seeing such food Bhai Mardana started to think. Guru Jee knew what he

2

was thinking and said, "Mardana, when you eat the food, then all will be revealed to you."

After saying this, Guru Jee gave Bhai Mardana some food to eat. When he ate this food, it tasted like immortal nectar (Amrit) to him. Guru Jee then said to Bhai Mardana, "Mardana - what sort of food was cooked and what sort of taste did you experience?"

Bhai Mardana replied, "The food tasted like Amrit (immortal nectar). You are the knower of hearts (antarjami) and all knowing."

Bhai Lalo said to Guru Jee, "Greatness is all yours, as you are great. You look at the heart-felt devotion and don't judge the food that is cooked. You have abolished the anguish of many lives of mine and have made all my efforts fruitful. You are forever merciful to your devotees." Saying this, Bhai Lalo bowed at the feet of Guru Jee. Guru Jee placed his hand upon his head (blessing him) with the placement of their hand – Bhai Lalo's ignorance was abolished. He became wise and all-knowing of all 3 worlds (Earth, Heaven and nether regions).

Bhai Lalo served Guru Jee with much love. Guru Jee stayed at his house for three days. From here, Guru Jee now wanted to travel further ahead. Bhai Mardana said, "You are the knower of hearts (antarjami). The people here have polluted minds and they slander us. Wherever I go, people say, 'That is the Marasi of the one who is treading the wrong path. Hearing this, I get angry. Guru Jee, let's leave here.'"

During the ambrosial hours (Amrit Vela), before dawn, Guru Jee made preparations to leave. Guru Jee said to Bhai Lalo, "May the creator Lord remain in your thoughts. We want to now travel more." Bhai Lalo said, "Why are you leaving my house? What have I done wrong? Know me to be your servant." Guru Jee said, "You have not done anything wrong. Seeing us, people are angered. You have the intellect of a saint; we are very pleased with you."

Bhai Lalo said to Guru Jee, "Please accept my humble request and stay at my home for at least one month more."

Guru Jee replied, "We cannot refuse your request."

Bhai Mardana Jee made a humble request to Guru Jee, "You are to stay here for a while. Grant me leave to see how my family are, in Talvandi and I will then return. When I am at Talvandi, what news shall I share with others about you?" Guru Jee said, "Just inform them of what you have witnessed." Bhai Mardana Jee left with the permission of Guru Jee.

After this, Guru Jee used to spend his days in the jungle and return to Bhai Lalo's home in the evening. Bhai Lalo Jee used to prepare food for Guru Jee with much love. Guru Jee is forever tied to the love of their devotees. Bhai Lalo Jee would do his work during the day; in evenings he would serve Guru Jee and listen to their words lovingly.

There is a Gurdwara called 'Gurdwara Bhai Lalo dee khooh' (well of Bhai Lalo) at the site of Bhai Lalo's house nowadays.

Revision Questions Chapter 1

1) Where did Bhai Lalo live and who was he?
2) When Guru Jee gave Bhai Mardana food, what did Bhai Mardana say? What did Bhai Lalo say?
3) When Bhai Mardana used to go out what would people say?
4) Bhai Mardana sought permission to go where?

Chapter 2
Malik Bhago's feast

When Guru Jee lived at Bhai Lalo's house, there was a minister of the Governor of Eminabad called Malik Bhago, who was a Khatri (warrior caste). He accumulated wealth by various sinful acts. He wanted to provide a feast for the local people with this money and become more famous in the area by doing so. With this in mind, he decided to conduct a 'Brahm Bhoj' (a ceremony in which 'Brahmins,' the priestly caste, are fed first and then others partake in the feast). Malik Bhago sent out a Brahmin to extend invites to all the local population to attend this feast. This Brahmin saw Guru Jee and said, "Please attend Malik Bhago's Brahm Bhoj and eat."

Guru Jee declined attending and said, "I am a Darvesh (a renunciate Saint – Saints that don't involve themselves in worldly affairs)."

The Brahmin said, "This is why people say you are treading on the wrong path (darvesh were mostly sufi saints – thus the Brahmin is trying to say Guru Jee has become a Muslim saint). If you do not attend, Malik Bhago will be angry with you."

After saying this, the Brahmin left.

Those who ate the food provided by Malik Bhago were very pleased and sang his praises. When the Brahmin saw that Guru Jee had not come to eat, he told Malik Bhago, "Nanak Tapa (meditative) has not come."

Upon hearing this, Malik Bhago was enraged and said to the Brahmin, "Go and call him right away." The Brahmin quickly went to Bhai Lalo's house, and upon seeing him, he said, "Where is Nanak Tapa Jee?"

"He is here", said Bhai Lalo.

Hearing this, Guru Jee came out and said, "Pandit Jee, what do you need from me?"

The Brahmin replied, "Malik Bhago has called for you."

Guru Jee replied, "I do not know Malik Bhago and have no reason to meet him."

Saying this, Guru Jee refused to go.

The Brahmin returned to Malik Bhago and exaggerated about what had happened. Hearing the words of the Brahmin, Malik Bhago was further angered. He now sent five other men with the Brahmin to get Guru Jee to come to him. Upon arriving at Bhai Lalo's house, the Brahmin said to Guru Jee, "Malik Bhago is very angry with you. If you do not go to him now, we will take you by force."

Hearing this, Guru Jee agreed to go – in order to teach Malik Bhago a lesson (who was amongst those people with a corrupt intellect). Bhai Lalo went along with Guru Jee. In the town there was much commotion about Nanak Tapa being ordered to come to Malik Bhago. Many people came to witness what would now occur.

Guru Jee asked Mailk Bhago, "Why have you repeatedly called me here?"

Malik Bhago replied, "I have organised a Brahm Bhoj. Why did you not come to eat? As a Khatri (warrior caste) you eat food at the house of a Shoodar (low caste). What fault do you see in the Brahm Bhoj that you refused to attend it."

Guru Jee said, "Bring a little food from your feast to me."

6

Malik Bhago ordered some food to be brought to Guru Jee.

Guru Jee said to Bhai Lalo, "Bring some food from your house, too."

Bhai Lalo quickly went and brought back some left over kodhre dee roti (chapatti made with finger millet flour).

Malik Bhago's food was fried in oil. Many different dishes were put into a tray and placed in front of Guru Jee.

Guru Jee now placed Bhai Lalo's chapatti in his right hand and the fried chapatti of Malik Bhago's in his left hand. Guru Jee squeezed them both firmly. Milk came out of Bhai Lalo's chapatti and blood came out of Malik Bhago's chapatti. People in the crowd were shocked when they witnessed this miracle. They said, "We have never ever seen anything like this before." The people saw what had happened, but nobody really understood why it had occurred.

Guru Jee said to Malik Bhago, "You have made many people suffer in your accumulation of wealth. It is from this money of suffering that you have organised this Brahm Bhoj. Eating this food destroys good actions. Those who do not know this, are happily drinking this blood of sin in the food. They are polluting their own minds by eating this food. Those who know of your sins – why should they consume this blood that you have gathered? Look within yourself and assess your sins. Look at the food from the house of the Shoodar (low caste), milk came out of it. Eating from Bhai Lalo's house is a daily Brahm Bhoj which is why I eat at his house. He makes food from an honest living. Malik Bhago, you are seeing your Brahm Bhoj and listening to your praises being sung – by which you are growing your ego."

Hearing all this, Malik Bhago burnt in rage and he had no reply. He hung his head in shame. However, his corrupt intellect still prevented him from falling at the feet of Guru Jee. Malik Bhago burnt with enmity.

Guru Jee left Malik Bhago's house and returned to Bhai Lalo's home. The people with good intellect praised Guru Jee. They would bow at Guru Jee's feet, wherever they met them. They would say, 'Guru Jee has much spiritual power. Whoever slanders them, will suffer.'

There were some people who were ignorant and did not want to know the greatness of Guru Jee.

Revision Questions Chapter 2

1) Who was Malik Bhago? With what desire did he conduct the Brahm Bhoj?

2) What happened when Guru Jee squeezed the chapattis of Malik Bhago and Bhai Lalo?

3) How did Guru Jee describe the accumulation of wealth by Malik Bhago?

4) How did Guru Jee describe the food of Bhai Lalo?

Chapter 3
Bhai Mardana eats poisonous fruit

Guru Jee bade farewell to Bhai Lalo and set off. Bhai Bala and Bhai Mardana were now both accompanying Guru Jee on their travels. Three days had passed in travel and Bhai Mardana became extremely hungry. He found walking difficult, as hunger was making his body weak. He thought, 'How will I manage to travel with them? They never get hungry. I will die of hunger.'

Guru Jee knew what Bhai Mardana was thinking and asked, "Bhai Mardana, how are you?"

Bhai Mardana replied, "You are the form of God. You don't get hungry. Hunger is making me suffer. Three days have passed without food. Like this, I will die of hunger any day."

Guru Jee said, "We will not let you die. Even if you die, we will revive you."

At that moment Guru Jee saw a crown plant and said, "Eat the fruit off this tree and expel your hunger."

Bhai Mardana said, "Are you teasing me? Are you trying to kill me by getting me to eat this fruit?" (Ak deea kakkria are poisonous, which are known as 'crown plants' in English).

Guru Jee said, "Eat to your full contentment. Obey our word. You will not experience any pain whatsoever."

Bhai Mardana obeyed Guru Jee and started to eat the fruit and he found them to be delicious. He ate to his full, but he still felt like eating more. Becoming greedy, Bhai Mardana broke some of the fruit off and hid it in his clothes to eat later (hiding this from Guru Jee). The next day, when Bhai

Mardana got hungry, he ate the fruit secretively. Immediately, he cried out in anguish and had his head down as he was in so much pain but he still could not tell Guru Jee the truth.

Guru Jee said to Bhai Mardana, "In greed, you hid the fruit - you didn't ask us to eat it with you. This is why you are in so much pain. If you had asked us to share it with you, you wouldn't have experienced this pain."

Bhai Mardana said, "I made a mistake unintentionally. I didn't realise your greatness. I ate them like before, thinking they would be sweet."

There was another crown plant nearby. Guru Jee broke fruits off it and gave them to Bhai Mardana to eat. When Bhai Mardana ate these fruits, all of his bodily pain disappeared. Bhai Mardana was now elated and clasped his hands. He bowed upon Guru Jee's feet. Guru Jee now travelled further ahead.

Revision Questions Chapter 3

1) When Bhai Mardana got hungry what did Guru Jee tell him to eat?

2) What did Bhai Mardana eat that made him ill and what cured him?

Chapter 4
Guru Jee goes to Kamru Desh

Sri Guru Nanak Dev Jee, Bhai Bala and Bhai Mardana went to Kamru Desh, which in modern day India is in Assam and is referred to as the Kamrup region. When Guru Jee visited this area, it was under incantations (spells) and various forms of black magic. Just outside the city, Guru Jee went and sat under the shade of a tree. Some time had passed after being seated here and Bhai Mardana asked, "My faithful Lord, I am extremely hungry. Give me permission to go and eat some food in the city."

Guru Jee replied, "Do not go to the city. It is full of sorrow."

Bhai Mardana said, "You don't eat or drink anything yoursef but are putting fear into me so I don't go to the city. Without food, my body is withering away."

Guru Jee said, "Ok, go and have a look in the city then."

Bhai Mardana went to the city to eat. In the city, he saw beautiful women, who were adorned with good clothes and jewellery. Whichever traveller came here, these women would put spells over them and get them to sin with them. These adulterous women also controlled their husbands so that they could sin with freedom.

When these women saw Bhai Mardana, one of them put a thread, which had a spell on it, over the neck of Bhai Mardana. Bhai Mardana was immediately transformed into a sheep. They put a rope over his neck and tied him to a post. Bhai Mardana couldn't do a thing and he started to think, 'I did not obey Guru Jee! That's why I am now stuck here. I cannot even speak to tell anyone of what is going on.' He thought, 'If Guru Jee knows everyone's thoughts then Guru Jee will come and save me.'

Guru Jee the knower of all said to Bhai Bala, "Let's go and free Bhai Mardana."

Bhai Bala asked, "Where is he?"

Guru Jee said, "Those women in the city have turned him into a sheep through their spells and he is tied to a post."

Bhai Bala said, "This is what he deserved, as he did not heed your advice. Let him suffer for a while. Do not free him quickly, so he realises his mistake fully."

Guru Jee said, "We brought him along and have to look after him. He cannot forego hunger. We have much use for him. He is remembering us. Come, let's go and free him."

Saying this, Guru Jee and Bhai Bala started out to go and free Bhai Mardana. Seeing Guru Jee from afar, Bhai Mardana was elated. He started signalling by moving and stamping his hooves. He then started to belch out as a sheep does. He moved his head up and down and stamped his hooves quickly on the ground.

Guru Jee went and stood outside the house where Bhai Mardana was tied. The women were very happy upon seeing Guru Jee. Two women came forward with strings in their hands and they were reading incantations (spells) as they walked forward. One of them was about to put a string over Bhai Bala's head but she immediately became a sheep. The second woman came forward to put the string over Guru Jee but she immediately became a female dog. The other women quickly ran indoors.

Guru Jee said to Bhai Bala, "Break the thread around Bhai Mardana's neck and bring it to me."

Bhai Bala did as he was told. Bhai Mardana immediately became human again. He came and bowed to Guru Jee and said, "I am simple as `I do not know deception."

Guru Jee said, "You did not obey our instruction."

Guru Jee was in conversation when the husbands of the women arrived. The women were still in the form of a sheep and a female dog - they immediately ran to their human husbands. They could not speak but were circling their husbands and pointing their tails towards Guru Jee, trying to signal what had happened.

Seeing their wives like this, the husbands understood what had happened. They thought, 'Our wives must have tried to put a spell over the Saints which has backfired. They must be a true Saint. We should seek forgiveness for our wives' mistakes.'

At this point, both the husbands fell at the feet of Bhai Bala who said, "Clasp the feet of Guru Jee and seek forgiveness. They are merciful."

Hearing this from Bhai Bala, they both fell at the feet of Guru Jee and asked for forgiveness for their wives. They said, "Relinquish your anger. Forgive their mistakes. They did not know your greatness. They have got the punishment for their sin. Great Saints are benevolent. You have no desires. Please bless them in your sanctuary and make them human again. Forgive their sin."

Guru Jee said, "Take on our teachings of Sikhi and build a Dharamsala (a place of worship and sanctuary) where you will conduct daily congregations (satsang) in the morning and evening. Here, you should serve Sikhs and Saints which will be for your betterment. At death, the death's angels will not then make you suffer. Give up your lives of sin and earn an honest living."

Hearing these words of Guru Jee, they accepted this advice and said, "We will do as you say."

Guru Jee said, "Punishing such women was appropriate. As you have accepted to give up lives of sin, I will now transfer them back to human form." The women then returned back into their normal bodies.

Night fell and Guru Jee spent the night there. Guru Jee woke up at Amrit Vela (the hours before dawn). Many people arrived with offerings to Guru Jee when they heard of the miracle of yesterday. Those with great fortune became the Sikhs of the Guru by taking initiation with 'Charan Pahul' (drinking water blessed with Guru Jee's feet). These Sikhs built a Dharamsala and daily sang the praises of Guru Jee.

Guru Jee stayed here for five days and then said, "We are to now travel further ahead."

All these new Sikhs clasped their hands and supplicated, "You blessed us all. You abolished our sinful intellect and put us on the path of love and devotion to God. Please stay for some more days."

Guru Jee replied, "Meditate on God daily, visit the Dharamsala daily and congregate. Make Karah Parshad (blessed communal offering made of flour, butter, sugar and water) and do Ardas (supplication prayer). By doing this, all your mind's desires will be fulfilled."

After giving these teachings, Guru Jee left.

Revision Questions Chapter 4

1) Where is Kamru Desh?

2) When Bhai Mardana went to eat in the city what happened?

3) When Bhai Bala and Guru Jee went to the city – what did the women do and what then happened?

4) What teachings did Guru Jee give the people?

Chapter 5
Guru Jee liberates Kauda Rakash

Sri Guru Nanak Dev Jee was liberating sinners and the cursed. They now arrived at Jabalpur (Madhya Pradesh), along with Bhai Bala and Bhai Mardana. Guru Jee sat down to rest here in a jungle.

Guru Jee has the power to do anything and Guru Jee purposely put a thought into the mind of Bhai Mardana, who said: "I am sad. I want to go and see my family. Grant me permission to leave."

Guru Jee warned Bhai Mardana, "Don't go. In the jungle there is a demon who will eat you."
Guru Jee repeatedly tried to convince him not to leave, but he stubbornly refused and was adamant to visit his family.

Guru Jee said to Bhai Bala, "If he listens to you, get him to stay here." Bhai Bala tried to convince him to stay but Bhai Mardana still refused. He said farewell to Guru Jee and left.

Guru Jee remained where they were, spending the rest of the day there. Bhai Mardana walked all day. At night he took rest somewhere. The next day, he set off again towards his home when, suddenly, a demon (Rakash) captured him and took him!

Now, other than Guru Jee, no-one else could save Bhai Mardana Jee, who was now fraught with fear; he trembled and went yellow with fear. He thought, 'Now, I will die.' He thought, 'Guru Jee is merciful and They will free me.' Thinking this, he now started to pray to Guru Jee to free him. At this point, Guru Jee said to Bhai Bala, "A demon has captured Bhai Mardana - the demon will fry him and eat him."

Bhai Bala said, "Guru Jee, you tried to stop him leaving but he didn't listen and was too attached to his family."

Guru Jee said to Bhai Bala, "Come, quickly! Let's go and save him. We have much use for him."

Bhai Bala said, "How far is the demon from here? Won't he eat Bhai Mardana before we arrive?"

Guru Jee said, "He is only 11 hours away." Saying this, Guru Jee held Bhai Bala by the arm and they arrived at where the demon was in a second.

Guru Jee said to Bhai Mardana, "Why are you sitting here? Why haven't you gone home?"

Bhai Mardana dropped his head in shame, but was so happy to see Guru Jee as he knew he would now be saved. Guru Jee said to Bhai Bala, "The demon is going to fry Bhai Mardana in this boiling oil and eat him. Let us stay out of sight."

Bhai Bala said, "If the demon eats Bhai Mardana then what was the point of us coming here? Please save him, somehow."

Guru Jee said, "You watch the entertainment for now."

The demon could not see Guru Jee but Bhai Mardana could. When the oil was burning hot like fire, the demon put Bhai Mardana into it. Bhai Mardana now screamed out and said, "Guru Jee, save me! I am at your mercy!"

When Bhai Mardana's body touched the oil, the oil became cool. Now, Guru Jee revealed himself to Kauda, the demon. Seeing Guru Jee, he asked, "Who are you? Where have you come from? You made my burning hot cauldron cool."

17

Guru Jee said, "Kauda, why did you take so long trying to eat him?"

Hearing this from Guru Jee, Kauda was shocked and he said, "How do you know my name? I have never met you before." Saying this, he now remembered his previous lives. With the sight of Guru Jee (darshan), his curse was now alleviated.

Kauda had a mirror. He brought that mirror out and put it in front of Guru Jee. When he saw Guru Jee's reflection, he became overwhelmed with love for Guru Jee and quickly fell at the feet of Guru Jee, bowing down to Them. He clasped his hands and stood upright.

Guru Jee said, "Tell us your story."

Kauda said, "Please grant me your permission to get you some sweet fruits from the jungle then I will tell you everything."

With Guru Jee's permission, he went into the jungle and returned with some sweet fruits, which he placed respectfully in front of Guru Jee.

Guru Jee said to Kauda, "Recognise Mardana as your Guru and bow down to him. You will then be liberated."

Hearing these words of Guru Jee, Kauda said, "He is my worshipable Guru. I have experienced much bliss upon meeting him." Saying this, he bowed at Bhai Mardana's feet.

Bhai Mardana was elated with all this and said, "Guru Jee, please keep me with you at all times."

Guru Jee said, "We are forever happy with you - stay with us. You are probably hungry. Eat these fruits."

Bhai Bala placed the fruits in front of Guru Jee for Them to eat first. Then Bhai Bala gave the fruit to Bhai Mardana. Bhai Bala ate some fruit himself. The fruit that was given to Guru Jee. Guru Jee gave it to Kauda to eat. When Kauda ate these fruits, his body was transformed from that of a demon into a handsome human.

Kauda now sang the praises of Guru Jee, "You are the creator of the universe and the nurturer of devotees to God. I bow to your greatness." He praised Guru Jee and bowed at Their feet again.

Kauda now said to Guru Jee, "Now, listen to my previous history. You are the knower of hearts (antarjami) but I will still narrate everything, as you have asked to hear it from me. In my last life I was a Brahmin. I became egotistical due to my studies and learning. One day, my perfect Guru who was one with God, came to my home. I was rude and did not show Them due respect. When They entered, I did not rise. My Guru got upset with this disrespect and cursed me, saying, "You have taken on the wrong intellect. Nothing will affect me but if you do not get the fruit of this disrespect then this good practice (of rising when more respected people enter the room) shall vanish from the world. For this reason, you shall now take on the body of a demon and undergo the consequences of your disrespectful actions."

Kauda said, "Hearing my Guru Jee's curse, I was stricken by fear and started to tremble."

I said to my Guru, "For my sin, I will now become a demon. Please tell me how long will I be in anguish in this demonic body?"

Hearing this, my Guru Jee became merciful, "God will come as an Avatar (incarnation) to the earth. They will liberate you."

I supplicated to my Guru Jee, "How will I know God has come to me? Please tell me."

Hearing this, my Guru gave me this mirror and he said, "The Avatars' face will reflect as a human being in the mirror. Those who have been through the cycle of births and death will show no reflection in the mirror when their faces are put in front of it."

I brought this mirror from my Guru and have been living here ever since. I brought many humans here and put their faces in front of the mirror and many showed reflections of pigs, dogs, birds and so forth, but your face reflected as that of a human in the mirror. By having your sight (darshan), my curse has been lifted. This is my story. You are the form of God. Grant me permission to go to Sachkand (realm of truth in the afterlife). I will now be happy forever as I have had your blessed sight (darshan). He bowed to Guru Jee and left for Sachkand. Seeing this miracle, Bhai Mardana fell at the feet of Guru Jee.

Bhai Mardana started to say, "You are great, you are great."

He asked Guru Jee, "Shall we take this mirror along with us?"

Guru Jee replied, "What use do we have for this mirror? Keep the mirror of contemplation within you, with which divine wisdom blossoms forward."

This historical occurrence is commemorated today at Gurdwara Marahatal MP SH 22 Marhatal Jabalpur Madhya Pradesh, today.

<u>Revision Questions Chapter 5</u>

1) In what sort of area did Guru Jee liberate Kauda? What is there today?

2) To save Bhai Mardana how far did Guru Jee travel in one second?

3) How did Kauda's boiling oil cauldron cool down? What did Kauda say when this occurred?

4) Describe what Kauda told Guru Jee about his personal history

5) The mirror that was given to Kauda by his Guru – what was special about it?

Chapter 6
The Emperor Karu

Guru Jee, along with Bhai Bala and Bhai Mardana, arrived at Rom Des. The Emperor Karu was the ruler at the time. The population there was suffering a lot due to poverty. They could not serve any saints or guests who visited their country.

To put Karu on the right path, Guru Jee went directly to the doors of his fort. Guards were at the doors. Guru Jee asked them, "How much charity does your king give? How does he ensure justice is adhered to?"

The guards replied, "Karu has made the population suffer a lot. He is a miser and a tyrant. He does not give even a little bit of charity. He has robbed the population of its wealth. His brother, Haru, accumulated a lot of wealth and put it in 40 treasure chests but through tyranny, Karu has increased this to 45 treasure chests. He does not listen to the pleas of anyone. For this reason, many have left the kingdom and others, crying out for help, have died destitute."

Guru Jee asked, "How did he accumulate his wealth? People hide their wealth. How did he
get money, jewellery or precious goods out of people?"

The guards replied, "Once, Karu called all his ministers to his court and told them to tell him where there was more wealth or there would be dire consequences." The ministers in fear replied, "We cannot even find a single rupee in the country even after searching for it."

Hearing this, Karu called his daughter and said to the ministers, "Announce to the whole country that whoever gives me 1 rupee, they will be married to my daughter."

His daughter was made to stand on a platform in the city. Hearing this, a youth came forward. Seeing the princess, he was attracted to her. He ran home and said to his mother, "Mother give me 1 rupee. I want to buy the King's daughter."

The mother replied, "Son, 1 rupee cannot be found even after extensive searches in our country. When we don't have money, why is Karu trying to get us to buy his daughter in such a manner?"

The son said, "If you do not give me 1 rupee, then my life will not be worth living." Saying this, he fainted and fell to the floor.

His mother cried a lot and said, "Son, get up and I will tell you how to get the money. When your father died, a rupee was put in his mouth when he was buried. If you cannot live without the princess, then dig up your father's grave and get the 1 rupee out from there."

Hearing this, the boy was elated. He went to his father's grave, extracted the 1 rupee and went straight to the king. He handed the payment over to get the princess. Seeing this, Karu was very happy and called the youth to his court.

Karu warned him, "Tell the absolute truth of where you got the money from because if you lie...I will kill you."

The youth said, "I got it from my father's grave. If you find any money in my house, you can kill me."

When Karu heard of this, he ordered for all graves to be dug up in order to remove the rupees from the dead. The guards now said to Guru Jee, "Oh Saint, there is no tyrant as bad as our King."

Guru Jee said, "He is an extreme sinner and he will go to hell."

Guru Jee now said to the guards, "Go and tell Karu there is a Sant at his doors who wants an audience with him. Tell him that I have no desire to ask him for anything. He should come out to meet me here."

The guards went to Karu, clasped their hands and said, "There is a Saint at your doors. He has no desire to ask you for anything (money, etc). He just wants an audience with you."

Karu came out with his advisers, bowed to Guru Jee and stood there. Guru Jee was collecting shards of pottery at the time and putting them in His satchel. Karu was shocked when he saw this and asked, "What will you do with these accumulated shards of pottery?"

Guru Jee replied, "We will take these shards with us into the afterlife."

Karu said, "Your human body does not go with you into the afterlife – how will these shards of pottery go with you?"

Guru Jee said, "The 45 treasure chests of wealth that you have amassed through sinful actions – how will they then go with you into the afterlife? Your brother, Haru, died amassing 40 treasure chests...nothing went with him at death. You have added another 5 treasures chests to this collection. Remember, none of this wealth will go with you at death. Then someone else will become the owner of it. They will then bury you. You will have to go through much pain in hell for your sins. If you want to better yourself, then stop sinning and being a tyrant. If you do not, then you will go to hell."

Having darshan of Guru Jee and hearing their words, Karu's heart melted and he spoke in humility: "What has come to pass, is in the past. Now, teach me how to tread the right path, with which I can have firm faith in God. My mind is forever thinking about wealth. I also cannot get rid of greed from my mind. Teach me how to destroy my sinful ways."

Guru Jee then uttered the Nasihatnama to teach Karu how to better himself (the Nasihatnama was not included in Sri Guru Granth Sahib Jee). Karu, upon hearing the Nasihatnama, was very scared as to what would happen to him in the afterlife and supplicated to Guru Jee, "I have sinned a lot. Bless me - make my life worthwhile."

Guru Jee said, "So long as you have the wealth amassed through sin in your possession, you cannot be freed from your past sins. Break your attachment to it. Due to wealth, our wives, husbands, children and social circle, become friends with us. When we have no wealth then no one asks after us. Everyone stays away. Worldly love is of no avail. Devotion to God forever provides peace/pleasure (Sukh). Forever love God."

When Karu heard these words he fell at Guru Jee's feet and said, "Whatever you instruct I will do that."

Guru Jee said, "Those people you have imprisoned – free them. Return the wealth of those you have taken it from. Whatever wealth is then left, spend it on propagating the name of God and on the poor. Forever meditate on God."

Karu said, "Now, I have been blessed. You are God themselves in human form…that is hiding in this form. With your grace, my greed has been dispelled. You have come to bless all of humanity."

Guru Jee stayed here for a few days and taught everyone to meditate on God then Guru Jee got ready to leave. Karu said, "The whole of the nation is your servant. If you must go, when will you return?"

Guru Jee said, "Keep God in your hearts and meditate. This is the way to meet me in the future, by meditating." Saying this, Guru Jee left.

Revision Questions Chapter 6

1) Why did Guru Jee go to King Karu?

2) Why were the population of Karu's kingdom suffering?

3) What did Karu say to his minister after calling his daughter there?

4) What did the youth ask off his mother? What did the mother say?

5) When the youth got the rupee and took it to Karu, what did Karu say?

6) When Karu came to Guru Jee what were they doing?

7) What was the name of the hymn Guru Jee uttered to teach Karu?

Chapter 7
The village that burns down

Sri Guru Nanak Dev Jee, Bhai Mardana and Bhai Bala went to a village that used to burn down every six months. Guru Jee went and sat under the shade of a tree when they arrived there.

The locals came and bowed down to Guru Jee, recognising Them as a Saint and offered them food to eat. Guru Jee spent some days here. Then one day, all the villagers loaded all their belongings on to carts and started to make their way to leave.

Guru Jee asked them, "What suffering is making you leave your village?"

The villagers replied, "This village burns down after every six months. The time is near for it to burn down again."

Guru Jee said, "If you become our Sikhs then your homes will not burn down. Meditate on God's True Name - abolish fear from your hearts. Dwell in your homes with peace."

Upon hearing these words, they were happy and they immediately took Amrit from Guru Jee's feet (charan pahul) and returned their belongings to their homes. Now, they all came and sat with Guru Jee, as they were still scared the fire might start again. Guru Jee got everyone to meditate on God's name.

Out of nowhere, a fearful demon appeared. In his hand he had fire. He said, "You stayed here and no longer fear me. I will not spare you now and will eat you."

The villagers said, "Before we were fearful of fire destroying our homes -now, we are too scared to die."

They went yellow in fear and said, "We were about to leave but these Saints stopped us."

Seeing the people tremble in fear, Guru Jee looked at the demon in anger. The demon immediately fainted. His head fell towards the feet of Guru Jee and Guru Jee felt mercy for him. Guru Jee put his foot on to the head of the demon. The demon then came about from being unconscious. Seeing Guru Jee's power, the demon was humbled.

The demon said to Guru Jee, "Forgive my mistake. You are the form of God. You have come disguised as a Saint. I am ignorant and did not know your greatness. I used to get these villagers to be under my control so that is why their homes burnt down. With your arrival, their great fortune has been awakened. You are benevolent. I am the slave of your slaves. Whatever you command me, I will do that."

Guru Jee said to the demon, "Build a Dharamsala (place of workshop) in this village. All of the village should congregate there to meditate and sing God's praises. All your sins will thus be abolished. Bring water by carrying it on your head (in pitchers) for the congregation and sing God's praises. Then you will get liberated."

The demon then built a Dharamsala on that very spot. Then he served the Sangat (congregation) with great humility. Guru Jee would now preach in this Dharamsala and Kirtan (hymn singing) would take place. Seeing all this, the villagers were shocked and said, "Look, Guru Jee got a hawk to serve small birds (meaning Guru Jee got the demon to serve them)."
Hearing the praises of Guru Jee, people from nearby villages started to come here to have darshan (blessed sight) of Guru Jee.

Guru Jee solidified the discipline of Sikhi here. People would say, "They are God incarnate."

Guru Jee stayed a few days here and then left.

Revision Questions Chapter 7

1) Why did the villagers get ready to leave?

2) What did Guru Jee say to the villagers to stop them leaving?

3) What did the demon say to the villagers?

4) Why did the demon fall unconscious? How did he come back around to consciousness?

5) What teachings did Guru Jee give to the demon?

Chapter 8
Panja Sahib

Guru Jee now arrived at Hassan Abdal which is a few kilometres from the River Sind (today, it's in the district Attock of Pakistan). Hassan Abdal is 45km from Rawalpindi on the road to Peshawar. Here, Guru Jee sat under the shade of a pippal tree (ficus religiosa tree) which was at the bottom of a hillock. After being seated here for a while, Bhai Mardana said, "Guru Jee, I am thirsty. Tell me where I can find water. You know everything."

Guru Jee said, "Climb this hillock. At the peak, a powerful Muslim saint resides there called Vali Kandahari. He has gathered water from waterfalls and made a man-made lake. Go and ask him for drinking water."

Bhai Mardana scaled the hillock slowly. It was a 2km journey. When he got to the peak, he greeted the Saint respectfully and asked him for water. Vali Kandahari asked, "Which country do you come from? Are you alone or are there others with you?"

Bhai Mardana replied, "I am from Punjab. I am travelling with Sri Guru Nanak Dev Jee as we preach. All Hindus and Muslims believe in Him. The Hindus call Him their Guru and Muslims see Him as their Peer (Saint). Many powerful people, who could perform miracles, have fallen at the feet of Guru Jee. I play the Rabab for Them. They are seated at the bottom of this hillock under the shade of a pippal tree. I have told you all about myself, now please give me water."

Vali Kandahari got angry, hearing the praises of Guru Jee. He said, "If he is a miracle worker, then why can he not summon water to himself where he is seated? It is right to give the thirsty water, but after hearing your words, I will not give you water."

After hearing this, Bhai Mardana left and came down the hillock and told Guru Jee everything that had happened. Guru Jee said, "He has a lot of pride in his mind. He cannot hear the praise of others. He is burning in the fire of jealousy."

Guru Jee now sent Bhai Mardana again to ask for water off Vali Kandahari and said, "Mardana, go in humility and ask him for water and drink it there."

Bhai Mardana scaled the hillock again, obeying Guru Jee's command and upon arrival, he said to Vali Kandahari, "Peer Jee, it is a great deed to give water to the thirsty. Please give me water to drink."

The Peer answered in anger: "You said Tapa Nanak has miraculous powers but he cannot source drinking water for you? I will never give you water."

Hearing these angry words, Bhai Mardana came down the hillock to Guru Jee once again.

Bhai Mardana now told Guru Jee all about the anger of the Peer. Now, the knower of hearts (antarjami), Guru Jee, hit his walking stick into the rocks of the hillock. Immediately, water sprouted forward from where Guru Jee had hit the rocks. All the water that the Peer had on the hilltop was now transferred below, to where Guru Jee was sat.

The Peer learnt of all that had happened through his own spiritual powers. To stop the water at the bottom, he now rolled a big rock down the hill. That rock uprooted trees and shoots on its way down as it went straight to where Guru Jee was seated. Guru Jee put his hand on it and stopped the rock before it touched any water. Guru Jee's hand became imprinted into this rock.

Vali Kandahari tried to push the rock further in to the spring of water through his powers (to stop the water supply) but the rock remained where it was, unmoving. Then Vali Kandahari realised Guru Jee is more powerful than him. He then came and fell at Guru Jee's feet and said, "Oh God, forgive my mistake. I did not know your greatness. Now, please teach me how to fulfil my life so the afterlife will be prosperous for me."

Seeing his faith, Guru Jee gave him some advice, "You are suffering due to your jealously of others, which is completely unfounded. You cannot achieve anything like this. Remain happy and remember God at all times."

Vali Kandahari happily accepted these teachings and bowed at the feet of Guru Jee. He now supplicated to Guru Jee, "Guru Jee bless me with water, also."

Guru Jee said, "The water from rainfall will always be bountiful to you. It will never run out (in the man-made lake)." This is true to this day. The water on the top of the hillock remains in bountiful supply. When the water is about to run out, it starts raining.

The Peer carried on living here and singing Guru Jee's praises. Guru Jee's handprint on the rock remains to this present day. Some slanderers of the Guru tried to destroy the handprint of Guru Jee from the rock by smashing the rock with hammers and chisels but the handprint just went deeper into the rock and did not disappear. The water supply in this spring is plentiful as it was then. This place came to be known as Panja Sahib (place where Guru Jee's hand/ Panja imprinted the rock). The handprint in the rock miraculously takes in all sizes, shapes, ages of handprints.

Revision Questions Chapter 8

1) When Bhai Mardana got thirsty, who did Guru Jee send him to and where?

2) Why did Vali Kandahari refuse to give Bhai Mardana drinking water?

3) Where did Vali Kandahari's collected water now go?

4) Why did Vali Kandahari roll the rock down the hill and what did Guru Jee do?

5) From where did Guru Jee give Vali Kandahari his water?

Chapter 9
Guru Jee goes to Kabul

On Their travels, Guru Jee arrived at the capital of Afghanistan, the city of Kabul. Guru Jee went to a mosque here. A Mullah came and asked Guru Jee, "Who are you and where have you come from? You look like a Hindu...this is a place for Muslims. Do not sit here – leave!"

Guru Jee replied, "Travelling, we have become tired. We will leave in the morning after staying the night."

The Mullah said, "Do not sit or stay here. I do not allow Hindus to stay here. Go some place else. Listen to me and leave. If another Muslim comes and sees you here, you will get forcibly removed from here. Hindus have no place in a Mosque. It is good for you to now leave; if you do not listen, then I will force you to leave by pushing you out."

Guru Jee laughed and said, "If you are so powerful then make sure that this Mosque does not move. If you cannot do this, then you are making false claims of being powerful. You prattle like the sound of an empty pitcher."

The Mullah said, "The Mosque is here and it will not go anywhere. You are trying to scare me with these threats."

The Mullah was now very angry. To destroy the anger of the Mullah, Guru Jee now sat on top of the Mosque and made the whole Mosque fly around the city of Kabul. Seeing this miracle, the Mullah was terrified. Everyone who saw this was amazed - they witnessed the Mosque in the air, flying about. Hearing about this, the highest ranking Minister of the city arrived quickly at the Mosque.

Everyone said, "He is a Saint or prophet, or God Himself."

Everyone now started bowing to Guru Jee from afar. The Qazi of the city now supplicated to Guru Jee, "Please bring the Mosque back down to its place and give us your blessed sight (Darshan)."

Hearing this, Guru Jee returned the Mosque back to its original site. Then a lot of the people from the city came to have darshan of Guru Jee. People bestowed gifts and bowed at Guru Jee's feet.

Guru Jee taught them all about Naam and said, "You should all meditate on God's name. All anguish is abolished by doing this. At death, only this will be of support to you. Serve Saints and great souls with devotion."

Hearing Guru Jee's words, they all attained peace and happiness. The Muslims asked for Guru Jee's shoes (kharavaa) as a memento of this visit. They were given the shoes and they worshipped them. After staying a few days, Guru Jee left.

When Guru Jee put the Mosque back in its original location, it was now facing the West. All Mosques are built to face the North. Some years later, a ruler noticed that this Mosque was facing the wrong direction, in terms of Islamic thought, so he constructed the Mosque to face the North again. But at night, after the building was completed, the Mosque once again turned to face the West. Even today, this Mosque faces the West.

Chapter 9 Revision Questions

1. Where is the Mosque located that Guru Jee got to fly in the air?

2. Why did Guru Jee make the Mosque fly in the air?

3. How did Guru Jee make the Mosque return to its original location?

4. What did the people ask off Guru Jee as a memento?

5. Why were they reconstructing the Mosque to face the North again? Did it then face the North?

Chapter 10
Guru Jee goes to the town of thieves

Sri Guru Nanak Dev Jee now arrived in a town of thieves. Whoever visited the town was robbed and murdered by the residents. To teach and reform these thieves, Guru Jee had come here.

Guru Jee transformed Bhai Bala into a young woman of 16 years old. Guru Jee was adorned in fancy clothes, pretending to be the husband of this young woman. It looked like they had just been married. Bhai Mardana acted like the couple's attendant.

Guru Jee now went to the home of one of the thieves. The thief was very pleased seeing Guru Jee and he welcomed them all in and served them. The thief said, "Come, please stay at my home. I will serve you."

Guru Jee agreed to stay here to rest. The thief now invited all of the other thieves to his home. They talked to each other and said, "His forehead is shining (Guru Jee's). He must have a lot of money and expensive possessions. At night, steal all of his possessions. We will come back in the morning and we can share the goods that are stolen."

After saying this, the thieves left. Night fell when everyone ate their evening meal and went to sleep. God made everyone sleep so soundly that no one work up during the night.

Guru Jee woke up before dawn (Amrit Vela) and left. The thieves were still sleeping. After Guru Jee left, they woke up and all the thieves came to the house where Guru Jee had stayed. The thieves of the town said to the homeowner, "The goods you stole off the visitors to your house, share them amongst us now."

The thief replied in shock and said, "I didn't wake up last night. They left whilst I slept."

The other thieves thought he was lying and they started to argue with him and said, "You have gained a lot of possessions from them. In greed, you are now hiding this. Do not make up excuses - share what you have like you have always done previously." Hearing these words, the homeowner swore on the name of the Saint he believed in, to prove that he was not lying. Then everyone believed him.

The thieves then set out to find Guru Jee and they found Their footprints and followed the trail. Four young men were dispatched to capture Guru Jee. After travelling about 1 km, they saw Guru Jee and one of them shouted out, "Where will you go now? Just stop where you are. You have stolen things from my house so we are now going to kill you."

When Guru Jee heard these words, They stood still and enquired: "What are you saying?"

One of the thieves replied, "Give us all your money and possessions…you tricked us! We will not let you live now. This is the way that we live. First, we kill the person then we take all of their possessions."

Guru Jee said, "If you have come to kill us then do not murder us but just leave our bodies in the open. Leave after cremating our bodies. Then you can leave with our money and possessions."

The thieves replied, "We can do this but how will we light the fire for your pyre? We have no way of starting the fire here. If we leave you alone, you will tell others of what we did."

Guru Jee said to them, "Look, there is smoke coming from that direction. Bring fire here from there, whilst we are still alive. Two of you go and fetch something burning from the fire and two of you stay here to guard us." The thieves did exactly this.

The two thieves who went towards the smoke saw people beating up a man. They were swearing at him and they had him tied up and were taking him forward. The two thieves kept their distance from these people. They got a stick to burn from the fire and returned.

The thieves then saw the same man who was being beaten and dragged forward now being carried respectfully in a carriage. The thieves were shocked when they saw this and they went forward and asked, "The same man you were beating is now being honoured to travel in a carriage. Why are you doing this?"

The men beating him were death's messengers (jamdhoots) and they replied, "He was a great sinner so we were beating him to put him in pain. When Sri Guru Nanak Dev Jee looked towards his funeral pyre, all of his sins were abolished and he now has great fortune. Thus, we are now taking him to the heavens in this carriage."

The thieves asked, "Tell us, who is Sri Guru Nanak Dev Jee?"

Death's messengers said, "You are taking fire for Them - that is Sri Guru Nanak Dev Jee."

Hearing this, the thieves were shocked and said, "We are cursed."

They ran back to where they left Guru Jee and they clasped at Guru Jee's feet with their hands and said, "You are the destroyer of all pains... please forgive us."

The returning two thieves now explained everything they had witnessed. Hearing this, the other two thieves also fell at Guru Jee's feet. They said, "We make a living from killing and robbing people. You are the provider of all pleasures (sukh). You did not show us your power. We have sinned. You are benevolent, please come to our town and bless us."

Guru Jee accepted their plea and now travelled back to their town with them. The four thieves now told everyone in the town of what had happened. They got Guru Jee to sit upon a raised platform. Everyone started making offerings and bowing to Guru Jee. They all said, "Bless us with your teachings. We were all sinning. With your grace, we have now been put on the right path."

Guru Jee said, "Give up the murder of others and start farming for a living. All the money and possessions gained from the money of sinful actions - give it all to other people. Earn an honest living with your own hands. Out of your earnings, do good and share with others. Make a Dharamsala (place of worship) in your village - feed the needy and Saints. Forever meditate upon God, which will eradicate all your sins. Before dawn (Amrit Vela) rise and meditate. During the day, do your work. In the evenings, congregate in the Dharmsala to meditate on God. Do these things and your lives will become worthwhile."

Everyone now gave away all their money and possessions, which had been gained through sinful actions. All the people started farming. They collectively built the Dharamsala. They all became immersed in the love of God and became devout. Guru Jee stayed here for a few days and then left.

Revision Questions Chapter 10

1) When Guru Jee arrived at the town of thieves, what did they transform Bhai Bala in to and what did they become themselves?

2) What did all the thieves advise the thief to do at night? (This is where Guru Jee slept the night)

3) When the thieves went to capture Guru Jee, what did Guru Jee say to them?

4) What did the thieves see when they went to get the stick with fire?

5) What teachings did Guru Jee give to the thieves?

Chapter 11
The Story of Shau Sohagan

Sri Guru Nanak Dev Jee now arrived at a town inhabited by Muslims near to Sialkhot (Pakistan). There lived a fake Saint (Fakeer) here. He used to hold a festival one day after the full moon (Chand Raat Dooj). People would come and make various offerings at this festival. Candles would be lit, drums played and people would have fun and be happy. The fake Saint would say that, "On this night of the second day after the full moon, God comes to me (Shau- meaning God)." He had named himself Shau-Sohagan, meaning wife of God. He had flags posted at doorways and he would dress with many ornaments and jewellery, like a newly-wed bride.

Guru Jee came here to stop this fake practise and arrived at the home of an elderly woman. Guru Jee asked her, "Mother, why is there all this commotion in the town?"

The woman replied, "There is a Saint called Shau-Sohagan who lives here. Today, there is a festival at his place."

Guru Jee said, "Come, let's see the festival of this Saint." Along with Bhai Bala and Bhai Mardana, Guru Jee left for there. When Guru Jee arrived, there were crowds and lots of people. No one was allowed inside the room where Shau-Sohagan was and everyone had to bow to him from outside.

When Guru Jee tried to go inside, the guards at the door said, "You are not allowed inside -everyone bows from here and fulfils their pilgrimage here."

Guru Jee said, "Tell the Saint that a Saint has come to see him. Tell him I long for his darshan (sight of him). If he were to allow us, I would like to see him in person to fulfil my pilgrimage to this site."

The guards went and asked Shau Sohagan, who replied, "No, no-one has permission to enter. Today my husband (God) is going to come. God is the only one I see today."

The guards came back and gave Guru Jee his reply. Guru Jee said to Bhai Mardana, "There is nothing here as it is all fake."

After Guru Jee said this and left there, a fight broke out. Many people were injured and some were killed. People started looting. The more powerful started looting the less powerful.

Some people now entered Shau Sohagan's room, too. There was a beautiful woman in bed with him. He was sleeping with her. Upon seeing this, people were angered! They beat him and threw him out. The people looted all of his belongings. The whole town learnt that he was a fake - he was slandered by all and he was now very sad and in much anguish. He realised that Guru Jee is a great Saint... he remembered how he had refused Guru Jee entry and realised this led to him being disgraced.

Guru Jee had left for somewhere else after blessing the residents in Shau-Sohagans town. They returned after some time had passed and it was again the second day after the full moon. They had come to now bless Shau-Sohagan and They stayed at the elderly woman's house again. This time, there was no festival being held. Guru Jee asked the elderly mother, "Why is there no festival being held by Shau-Sohagan today? Is he here or not?"

The mother replied, "He was exposed as a fake Saint and no one believes in him now."

Hearing this, Guru Jee came out of the house. A physically disabled man was passing by. Through having the sight (darshan) of Guru Jee, he was cured of his disabilities. He fell at Guru Jee's feet and said, "I have been cured by your darshan." He sang Guru Jee's praises, uttering many kind words in gratitude. Guru Jee said to the man, "Go into the town and if anyone asks how you were cured, say Shau-Sohagan blessed you. He obeyed Guru Jee and did just this. This news spread quickly throughout the town. Shau-Sohagan also heard of this and he asked the man how he was cured and he also said to him that Shau-Sohagan cured him. Shau-Soahagan was shocked when he heard this from the man himself. He started thinking, who is the true Shah-Sohagan who cured him? He wanted to meet the real person who cured the man so he said, "Take me to the person who cured you."

The man brought Shau-Sohagan to Guru Jee. Shau-Sohagan now realised that this is the same Saint he had refused from his door. He fell at Guru Jee's feet and did not lift his forehead for a long time. He supplicated to Guru Jee, "You are the form of God. I mistakenly disrespected you. Please forgive me. I am your slave. You are my master. You have hid your greatness and given me praise (for curing the man)."

Guru Jee said, "The husband Lord (Shau) is present in all. Now, let everyone meet you and you openly meet all, too, and forever be devoted to God." He obeyed Guru Jee and was forgiven. He became Guru Jee's follower and people started to believe in him again.

People would now say, "We slandered him by mistake. The Shau (Husband Lord God) must surely come to him, as that is how he must have cured the disabled man. In this way, the respect and fame returned and the festival started to take place again.

44

Revision Questions Chapter 11

1) What did Shau Sohagan say to people about himself?

2) When Guru Jee tried to visit Shau-Sohagan in person - what was the reply?

3) When Guru Jee left the festival what happened there?

4) When people forced their way in to Shau Sohagan's room, what did they see?

5) When Guru Jee returned to the town- how did Guru Jee bless Shau Sohagan?

Chapter 12
Guru Jee's amazing words

Guru Jee now arrived at the village Kanganpur, which is in the district of Kasur in Pakistan. The residents here were very egotistical and sinful - they behaved badly towards everyone that they met. They did not know how to serve guests. If a traveller or someone would pass through their village, they would not be respectful to them; they would be rude and disrespectful.

When Guru Jee, Bhai Bala and Bhai Mardana arrived here, they were shown no respect by the villagers. They weren't offered any food or drink, nor anywhere to be seated or take some rest; instead, the villagers threw stones at them so they would leave. Guru Jee did not curse them but rather said, "Oh villagers, my friends - stay residing here." Today, there is a Gurdwara here called Gurdwara Mal Jee Sahib, it marks the spot where Guru Jee sat under a tree whilst being there.

Guru Jee travelled 2km further and arrived at the village Manakdeke. The people here were of a very good nature. They would serve guests who came to their village and helped everyone as much as they could. They served Guru Jee with great passion. When leaving the next day, Guru Jee said, "Oh villagers, you should disperse."

Hearing the words of Guru Jee, Bhai Mardana was shocked and said, "Guru Jee, you are uttering extraordinary words for people who showed us no respect, nor offered us food or drink. Instead of offering us somewhere to sit, they threw stones at us. You blessed them by saying, 'stay residing here'. But the good people who served us, you said to them, 'Become dispersed' – what did you mean by all this?"

Guru Jee said, "Whatever we have said, we have said it for the betterment of all. The people of the first village are sinful, wherever they go, they will spread their negativity and get others to do sinful things, thus they should stay where they are. This will be for the betterment of all (so these villagers do not disperse). The people of the second village are good natured. Wherever they go, they will guide people to do good things. It is for the betterment of all that these good people disperse into other villages, thus they will spot people doing bad things and get them to do good wherever they go. That's why I said they should disperse."

The people who threw stones at Guru Jee are famous for being diseased with Gilar/Goitre (enlargement of thyroid gland) – even today these families suffer from this disease. In the whole of Punjab, this is the only place known to constantly have this disease.

The village Manakdeke has a little habitation today in line with Guru Jee's words that all the villagers should disperse. Here Gurdwara Manji Sahib stands.

Revision Questions Chapter 12

1) What were the people of Kanganpur like? How did they serve Guru Jee?

2) What were the people of Manakdeke like? How did they serve Guru Jee?

3) Why did Guru Jee say 'disperse' and 'stay residing here' to the different villagers?

Chapter 13
The Kingdom of Kaval Nain

Guru Jee was travelling around the world with Bhai Bala and Bhai Mardana. Bhai Mardana said, "I am hungry, Guru Jee." As he said this, a tiger was seen. Guru Jee went towards the tiger and sat down in the same garden where the tiger was. Guru Jee said to Bhai Mardana, "Go and eat."

Bhai Mardana replied, "I have no money. How will I get food without money?"

Guru Jee replied, "I give you the whole city - it is yours so just go and eat there."

Bhai Mardana made his way into the city and saw great bazaars (shopping precincts), great desserts and cooked foods. He approached a man and asked, "What is the name of the king of this city? What is the name of the city? How does this city function?"

The man replied, "The name of this place is Swaranpur and there is no king like our king. You cannot buy anything here as there are no prices. Whatever one needs, they take without payment. These desserts that you see in the shops are given out free, as part of our faith. The King's name is Kaval Nain."

Hearing this, Bhai Mardana was pleased and said, "I am hungry and I am going to eat. Please tell me your name."

The man replied, "My name is Dharam Singh, whatever you desire, eat from these shops because no one will stop you."

Bhai Mardana said, "Give me the food with your own hands and I will then eat it."

Dharam Singh said, "Come, I will get your food. Take food for anyone else travelling with you, too."

Bhai Mardana said, "I have two companions travelling with me. They do not eat or drink anything. Just get food for me."

He got food for Bhai Mardana from a shop. Bhai Mardana ate the food and then toured around the city. Then he returned to Guru Jee. Guru Jee asked, "What sort of city did you witness? Did you manage to eat or not?"

Bhai Mardana said, "How can I describe the greatness of this city – I have seen no other like it. All of it is made of gold, the shops cook great food. They take no money for the food. I met a man who was very good natured. He got me food from a shop and told me to get food for my companions, too. I told him my two companions are content with not eating or drinking anything. After eating, I toured the whole city."

Guru Jee replied, "That is good - your desire was fulfilled."

Bhai Mardana enquired, "What sort of actions do the people of this city commit for them to live in such happiness?"

Guru Jee replied, "No one sins here. There is a big Dharamsala (place of worship) here. Sin has left the whole nation. The residents here are content and honest, living sinless lives. They all love doing good actions."

Bhai Mardana said, "You have described extraordinary traits and a new way of living has been described. I have never seen or heard of any place like this before."

Guru Jee said, "The ways of God are extraordinary. They are beyond our understanding. In kaljug, there is no comparable life to this one. Seventeen other kings have sworn allegiance to this kingdom. The king here is very righteous."

Bhai Mardana said, "Guru Jee, let's stay and live here. Here, we can get delicious cooked food."

Guru Jee said, "We are not in control of this. Wherever God takes us, we go there."

Guru Jee passed seven days seated there. Bhai Mardana would go to the city in the mornings and evenings to eat. Bhai Mardana put on weight with all the food he had been eating. One day, Bhai Mardana met Dharam Singh and he asked, "I have never seen your companions in the city. Where do they eat their food?"

Bhai Mardana replied, "They do not eat as they are content like this. If someone brings them food with devotion, then they eat it. They are seated in that garden."

Hearing this, Dharam Singh thought, "I should get darshan (blessed sight) of such Saints."

So Dharam Singh went along with Bhai Mardana. Dharam Singh lovingly brought a platter of food for Guru Jee to eat. He put the food in front of Guru Jee, bowed at Their feet and said, "Please eat this food and accept my offering; I have come after hearing of your greatness."

Guru Jee said to Dharam Singh, "Who has sent this food? Who are you and for what purpose have you come?"

Dharam Singh replied, "You are the giver of liberation. It has been seven days since you arrived yet you haven't eaten or entered the city. After hearing about you from your companion (Bhai Mardana), I have come to you. The king of our city, Kaval Nain, is righteous and free of ego. He does not show his prowess to anyone. Seventeen other kingdoms have voluntarily accepted his rule over them and they send him tribute (tax). I have narrated about myself – now, please eat the food I have brought."

Guru Jee said, "I have seen one fault in your king. For this reason, I will not eat this food. Where we see no fault, we only eat there."

Dharam Singh said, "I know of nothing like this. Please, tell me what you mean?"

Guru Jee said, "The person with the fault within them knows themselves what this is."

Dharam Singh bowed to Guru Jee, left and went to his King and said, "There are three renunciate saints here. One of them comes into the city and eats but the other two are in the garden and haven't eaten food for seven days. I took food for them to eat but they refused it as they said the King was at fault but they did not tell me what they meant by this."

The King was shocked upon hearing this and he thought, "What sort of saints are they, who have been seated outside the city for seven days?" Dharam Singh brought the King to Guru Jee, who brought along a gift for Guru Jee. Minsters and soldiers accompanied him. The King bowed to Guru Jee and came and sat near them. He asked Guru Jee, "Tell me what fault of mine have you seen?"

Guru Jee said, "If you see all humans as equal, then why are you getting other kingdoms to be subservient to you? The pride of your mind has not been abolished. The one who defeats ego is the true warrior."

The King replied, "I do not say anything to anyone. The Kings voluntarily became subservient. If you know I have ego inside me then please do abolish it."

Guru Jee said, "If you want to get rid of your ego then accept the king Sudar Sain as your superior (become aligned as an inferior king to him). Then we will accept you have no faults. Sudar Sain is a more powerful King than the 17 kingdoms aligned with you."

The King was delighted at hearing these words of Guru Jee, and responded with: "If you order me, I am willing to bow at the feet of the dogs of Sudar Sain."

Hearing this, Guru Jee was delighted, too, and said, "King, you are great. Your greatness is parallel to that of King Janak (an ancient famous saintly king). By serving him, you obtained this gift."

The King said, "If you know about my previous life, then please tell me more. Explain how I served King Janak and what I was blessed with. You are a perfect saint and I have had the good fortune to meet you."

Guru Jee said, "When King Janak was ruling, you were then called Safachand. You used to serve the king with much passion. One day, the King said, "I am thirsty. Bring me cold water from the mountain of ice, quickly." You obediently left to fetch the water. On the way there, you thought, 'If I were to be the King of a nation, I would also command such things and be happy. I would ask my attendants to get me whatever I desired.' Having thoughts like this, you brought the water. The King was happy when he drank the cool water and he said, "Ask for whatever you desire." You replied, "I have no desire." You did not reveal your true thoughts and did not ask for anything. The King knew your thoughts and said, "On the way to fetching water, in your thoughts you already asked for what you desired." At that time, the King Janak gave you a boon: that you will become a greater king than he was, you clasped both of your hands and said, "I served you to get wisdom of the soul (Atam-Gian). I have remained empty of that. The King replied, "In kaljug, you will meet the perfect Guru. You will achieve the wisdom of your soul from Them."

Hearing his previous history, King Kaval Nain was very happy. He fell at the feet of Guru Jee and said, "No one is a greater Guru than you. By having your darshan, all anxieties and anguish have left me. Please put your blessed feet in the palace and purify it." Guru Jee then went to the palace and stayed there for a while. The King served Guru Jee with a lot of passion. Guru Jee blessed the King with the wisdom of his soul and got him to meditate on God twice, daily. In the Dharamsala, Simran would now occur in line with Guru Jee's wishes where it was done both in the mornings and evenings.

Guru Jee got ready to leave there and the King said, "Let me also go with you. I will appoint someone else as the King."

Guru Jee said, "No, practice Raj-yoga (live in the kingdom and remain detached) and forever remain attached to God. We are always with you." Thus, giving the King patience to stay, Guru Jee bid farewell.

Revision Questions Chapter 13

1) Which kingdom did Kaval Nain rule? How many kingdoms were under his control?

2) What did Dharam Singh say to Bhai Mardana about buying food and what did Bhai Mardana say back?

3) When Bhai Mardana returned after eating, what did Guru Jee tell him about the king and kingdom?

4) When Dharam Singh took food for Guru Jee, what did Guru Jee say?

5) What did Guru Jee tell Kaval Nain about his previous life?

Chapter 14
Guru Jee goes to Mecca

Mecca is in Saudi Arabia. After Guru Jee left Kaval Nain's kingdom, Bhai Mardana said, "Guru Jee, Muslims praise Mecca and Medina a lot. Take me there, too."

Guru Jee replied, "Getting to Mecca from here will take us some years."

Bhai Mardana said, "You are all powerful - you can take us there in a second."

Listening to Bhai Mardana's plea, Guru Jee got them to Sukkur in minutes, which is in modern day Pakistan in the Sindh province. Upon arriving here, Guru Jee donned blue clothes. Guru Jee put a book under Their armpit. They put a Janeo (Hindu sacred thread) around their neck and wore a seli topi, a traditional woollen cap, upon their head. They put a frontal mark (tilak) upon their forehead. They gave Bhai Bala a Lota (a water carrying pot) and a prayer mat to carry. To teach the people here, Guru Jee was dressed partially as a Hindu and partially as a Muslim on Hajj (Muslim pilgrimage to Mecca). No-one could work out if Guru Jee was a Muslim or a Hindu. There were many Muslims here, ready to go on the Hajj (pilgrimage to Mecca) from around the world. These Hajjis (pilgrims) were going to Mecca by boarding a boat on the Indus River, which would transport them to Mecca via the sea. They were staying here to pass the night. Guru Jee went to these Hajjis, Bhai Bala spread out the prayer mat and Guru Jee sat upon it.

Seeing Guru Jee dressed like this, the other Hajjis were angered. They questioned Guru Jee, "Which country have you come from? Are you a Hindu or a Muslim? You are dressed like a Hajji but you have a tilak (frontal mark) upon your forehead."

Guru Jee said, "We have come from the country of Begampuru (the land without worries). I bear witness to both Hindus and Muslims. Humans have come to earth to immerse themselves in devotion to God. But both Muslims and Hindus have taken up half- baked intellect, forgetting God and being stuck in ego and claims of superiority. For these reasons, people become possessed with materialism and behave like animals."

The Hajjis said, "He is speaking great words. He must be a great Saint (Peer)."

They questioned Guru Jee further by asking, "This book you have on you - do you know how to read it or not? Tell us the meanings of the writings within it."

Guru Jee replied, "There are three ways to read a book. Like eating a bone, eating meat and eating seeds. To read a book and then enter needless debates about its contents, is like trying to eat a bone. To read a book and then become respected and get others to serve you, is like eating meat. Those who read it then meditate on God's name, those who see God in all and pray for the betterment of all, those readers are like those eating seeds."

Guru Jee said, "Know my name to be Nanak and we are going to Mecca."

Hearing this, the Hajjis thought, 'This is an intelligent Hindu. He wants to go to Mecca with us. Let's separate him from our group and not take him with us' Everyone spent the night here. In the morning, the Hajjis boarded the boat and left, leaving Guru Jee behind.

Guru Jee asked Bhai Mardana, "Is it not allowed for Hindus to go to Mecca?"

Bhai Mardana replied, "Nobody in the three worlds can stop you going anywhere. Be merciful and take me to Mecca and Medina, too." At this point, the boat had departed for the Hajj, so Guru Jee and his companions were now stranded here without any means to now get to Mecca.

Guru Jee said to Bhai Mardana, "If you are adamant you want to go then do Kirtan."

Bhai Mardana was happy hearing this and started to do Kirtan, singing a Shabad (hymn). When he finished singing the Shabad, he bowed at Guru Jee's feet. When he lifted his head, he could see the minarets around the city of Mecca.

Bhai Mardana now asked Guru Jee, "Where are we? What is this place?"

Guru Jee said, "Mardana, this is Mecca. We have come to fulfil your desire of pilgrimage here. Get up and have a look around."

Hearing this, Bhai Mardana was very pleased and they started walking forward together. The Kaaba had a boundary wall around it.

Guru Jee said to Bhai Mardana, "That which you had great desire to see, now go and see it." Obeying Guru Jee, Bhai Mardana went to have sight of the Kaaba. There were guards posted at the entrance of the Kaaba. They said to Bhai Mardana, "You do not have permission to go inside. If you want to go inside, you can go in after we blindfold you or just bow here and leave." Hearing this, Bhai Mardana returned to Guru Jee.

Guru Jee enquired, "Mardana, have you seen the Kaaba now?"

Bhai Mardana said, "The guards only allow you in blindfolded, otherwise you are not allowed to go and see inside. I have come with you. If I don't go inside and see what is inside the Kaaba, I will have doubts about what it is really like inside. Why do Muslims pray to it? I want to know the reason for this. If I do not see the inside of the Kaaba now, when will I see it? Oh my beloved God (to Guru Jee), please show me the inside of the Kaaba before we leave."

Guru Jee replied, "If you really want to see it, then go now. The guards will not see you."

Bhai Mardana now happily entered the Kaaba. No-one saw him enter. Bhai Mardana only saw a single black stone inside. After seeing this, he returned to Guru Jee.

Guru Jee enquired, "Has your desire now been fulfilled?"

Bhai Mardana replied, "I saw a black stone inside - tell me about it. Why is it seen to be so special? Why do people go inside blindfolded? Muslims are against stone idol worship. But here everyone is praying to a stone. You know everything, please bless me and tell me about all these things."

Guru Jee said, "They hide this truth. I will now narrate the history of this. This stone is a Shiva-ling (a stone of the sexual organ of Shiva Jee, the angel of death) and it has been here for a very long time. First, there was a jungle here and no temple or building existed. In this country, there was a King called Kunkaar. Seeing this stone, he was enraged. He got one of his servants to throw the stone idol far away and a fire then broke out, entrapping the whole kingdom. Many cities burnt down in the blaze.

The king then relinquished his pride and bowed to the Shiva-ling and begged for forgiveness. He believed the fires broke out in his kingdom as he had thrown the Shiva-ling out. When the King slept at night, Shiva Jee came to him in a dream and said, "Build a temple and place this Shiva-ling in it. Make people only enter when they are blindfolded or with their eyes shut. All your affairs will then be accomplished. Whoever enters without their eyes shut or covered, will be blinded."

In the morning, the King started the construction of the temple. This Shiva-ling has been here ever since. Shiva Jee showed his prowess and got this place built.

Guru Jee said, "The attendants of the Kaaba wash the Shiva-ling with water and the water that comes out of the Kaaba is then drunk by Hajjis- they believe it to be Amrit (nectar of immortality) and they believe all their sins are abolished by drinking it."

Bhai Mardana said, 'But I did not go blind by looking at it. Please explain why this happened. Why do Muslims also see Hindus as Kafirs (infidels) and lower than themselves?"

Guru Jee said, "They are Kafirs themselves, but call others 'Kafirs'. You are blessed by God that's so why you didn't go blind."

In this way, the day passed. At night, Guru Jee lay down with Their feet towards the Kaaba. When it was Amrit Vela (before dawn), a person called Jeevan came to sweep up. He was very angry with Guru Jee so he kicked Them and said, "Where have you come from? Do you know nothing? You have put your feet towards the temple of God. Have you no shame? Are you a Hindu or a Muslim? Get out of here!"

Guru Jee replied to Jeevan, "I am tired from travelling. I do not know in which direction my feet should face. Move my feet to the direction in which God's house is not."

Hearing this, Jeevan grabbed Guru Jee's feet violently and dragged them to the opposite direction. Now, the Kaaba moved to the direction in which Guru Jee's feet were moved to; wherever Jeevan would move Guru Jee's feet, the Kaaba would also follow. When the Kaaba moved like this, a crack appeared in it (which is even present today. That crack does not come out even though they have tried to repair it).

Jeevan now said, "I now know all about you. You are a Hindu - why have you come here?"

In the morning, a lot of Mullahs arrived (Muslim priests). They saw that the Kaaba had moved and were all shocked. They asked, "What is the cause of the Kaaba moving?"

Jeevan said, "At night, a Kafir was sleeping with his feet towards the Kaaba. I repeatedly told him not to put his feet in the direction of the Kaaba but he did not listen. So, I grabbed his feet and dragged them to another direction, but the Kaaba also moved to where his feet were pointing towards. He has done some sort of incantation or spell. He has great powers. I do not know anything more about him. I do not know if he is a Muslim or a Hindu. I could not tell. Come and see him."

The Mullahs were shocked when they heard Jeevan's account and they went and sat around Guru Jee. They asked, "Are you a Hindu or a Muslim? Putting your feet towards the Kaaba for Muslims is not allowed."

Qazi Rukadeen (a Muslim priest) asked Guru Jee, "Do you believe in the prophet Mohammed? Do you believe in God?"

Guru Jee replied, "In God's court, there are many prophets and saints standing with their hands clasped. We cannot count them all. Those who have forgotten the path to God, we have come to put them back upon it. You have forgotten the teachings of all the prophets. You have a superiority complex - you think your religion is the best. We will show you the correct path. If you do not accept it, you will go to Hell."

The Qazis now collectively asked Guru Jee, "Tell us who is greater, Hindus or Muslims? You have shown a great miracle here. No-one has witnessed such a miracle before. The Kaaba has moved with the movement of your feet. You are the Saint of all Saints."

Guru Jee said, "We all have bodies made of the five elements. We all have similar daily actions. Foolish people develop jealously and needless conflicts. No-one has imbued God's name in their mind; but by mediating upon God, we get liberated from this world. Without good virtues, both the religious and non-religious people end up in hells. The actions we commit for family wealth, cause us to go to many hells. People of the world only love us until we are alive in our human bodies. At death, no one is your friend, or of help. Our actions (karma) are always with us. God has different names in different religions. All these names refer to the same one God. Without meditating upon God, all will go to hells and suffer."

Hearing Guru Jee's words, all the people gathered at Their feet. Seeing Guru Jee as the form of God, they devoutly served Them. Guru Jee stayed here for quite a while.

Revision Questions Chapter 14

1) Where is Mecca?

2) How many different readers of scriptures did Guru Jee describe? Explain each one.

3) When Bhai Mardana went inside the Kaaba, what did he see?

4) How did Jeevan treat Guru Jee and what happened?

5) What did the king Kunkaar do to the Shiva-ling? What happened as a result of this?

6) What did Shiva Jee say to the king in his dream?

Chapter 15
Guru Jee goes to Medina

Guru Jee passed some time at Mecca and then asked Bhai Mardana, "Where do you now wish to go to?"

Bhai Mardana replied, "Please take me to the tomb of the Prophet Mohammed in Medina. We have come to this country; we can go there now and you always fulfil my desires."

Guru Jee said, "Medina is twelve days travel from here."

Bhai Mardana said, "It is not too far - we can arrive there quickly."

Guru Jee said, "Twelve days travel is a very far distance."

Bhai Mardana said, "Oh my beloved! With your blessings, we have travelled thousands of miles quickly – for that reason, I do not see it as being far away. You are the form of God who has come to liberate people on earth in Kaljug (present era of sin)."

Guru Jee said, "We will not refuse your request. We will take you to Medina."

In twelve days, they arrived at Medina. Guru Jee said to Bhai Mardana, "We have arrived at Medina. You wanted to see Medina: now, go and see it."

Bhai Mardana replied, "Oh my beloved, the guards will turn me away. How will I see it?"

Guru Jee said, "Here, they do not get you to close your eyes or blindfold you. You have the look of a Muslim anyway; no-one will stop you here."

Bhai Mardana said, "I am born in the home of Muslims but I am not one of them. I am your companion and a Sikh. I am in the sanctuary of your feet."

Guru Jee said, "If you believe this firmly then why did you want to go to Mecca?"

Bhai Mardana said, "I did not come to Mecca for worship. I only came to see what was here, due to the praise that Muslims give it. I see the faith of Muslims as inferior."

After saying this, Bhai Mardana went to see the Prophet Mohammad's tomb which was in a room. Afterwards, Guru Jee also went to the tomb. There were lots of Muslims priests serving the site. Seeing Guru Jee, they asked, "Who are you? You have come here wearing shoes. Are you stupid? This is not the way to make a pilgrimage. You have disrespected the Prophet Mohammed. Get back from here immediately."

Hearing these words, Guru Jee spoke a Shabad and the Prophet Mohammed's tomb came forward and lowered itself to Guru Jee's feet. Then, it went back to its normal site. Even today the tomb is slightly slanted at the same angle. The priests were shocked when they saw this miracle. They all now saw Guru Jee as the form of God and said, "We all saw the Prophet Mohammed as the greatest. If his tomb has bowed to you, we should, too."

They all came and bowed at Guru Jee's feet and got Guru Jee seated on a raised platform. They said to Guru Jee, "Give us your guidance."

Guru Jee said, "Remember your death at all times. Relinquish sin and see God in all, view everyone equally. Meditate on God's name. You will then not enter hells. Give up hypocrisy or outwardly appearances, commit yourselves to true devotion to God's name; by doing this, you will experience pleasure in everything you do."

Everyone was happy after hearing these words of Guru Jee. The attendants of the tomb asked for Guru Jee's shoes (Karava). They put the shoes near the tomb of the Prophet Mohammed so they could worship them, too. Guru Jee spent some days here and then returned to Mecca.

The Hajjis, who Guru Jee had previously met at Sukkur, now also arrived at Mecca. They were shocked when they saw Guru Jee (as they had left in their boat without them) and they asked, "When did this Hajji arrive here? We left him behind. How did he travel all this way before us? He seems to definitely be a Hindu."

The people who they were asking replied, "They have been here for a year. They have many powers and are the form of God. The Kabba even moved in the direction of their feet."

Hearing this, all these Hajjis now went and fell at the feet of Guru Jee and realised Guru Jee's greatness. They now wanted to see this power themselves, too, and they said, "If Guru Jee is God then They should provide us with water here."

Guru Jee had a stick and They hit it with great force into the wall of the Kaaba and water now started flowing from the hole that was created. They all did their ujju (ritual washing) with the water washing their hands, feet and faces. They fell at Guru Jee's feet once again.

Guru Jee, said, "Your Prophet Mohammed ate only jau (oats) here, whilst he meditated. Angels came to him and he became a true Prophet."

Everyone was pleased at hearing these words of Guru Jee. All the Muslims here started to serve Guru Jee and started to meditate like Guru Jee taught them. The priests said, "Give us your shoes for us to worship."

These shoes were put inside the Kaaba. The priests said, "God came in human form to liberate us." (Referring to Guru Jee's visit).

Revision Questions Chapter 15

1) Why did Bhai Mardana say 12 days journey was not far to travel?
2) How did the Prophet Mohammed's tomb show Guru Jee respect?
3) What teachings did Guru Jee give to the attendants of the Medina tomb?
4) Where did Guru Jee hit his stick to get water to appear?

Chapter 16
Guru Jee goes to Haridwar

Haridwar is a holy city of the Hindus. The River Ganga (Ganges) flows through it and it is viewed as a great 'Teerath'-site of pilgrimage that people bathe at. Guru Jee now arrived here and there was a festival taking place. Thousands of Hindus had converged on the city to wash their sins away by bathing in the River Ganga.

Guru Jee stayed the night here. In the morning, many people were standing in the river facing the sun and throwing water in its direction. Guru Jee entered the river and started throwing water in the opposite direction. People gathered around Guru Jee as they had never seen anyone throw water in this direction. Some were laughing and joking about Guru Jee's actions, some were asking Guru Jee if he was a Muslim or a Hindu. They enquired further to ask if he was a Muslim and to ask: why did he come to bathe in the River Ganga? They asked Guru Jee if he was a Hindu; why was he throwing water towards the West? What was the reason for this?

Guru Jee asked them, "First, you tell me as to why you are throwing water towards the East? Who is receiving this water?"

The people replied, "We are giving water to our deceased ancestors by throwing it towards the Sun."

Guru Jee asked, "How far away are your ancestors?"

The people replied, "Millions of miles away."

Hearing this, Guru Jee started throwing water towards the West again. The people asked, "You didn't explain yourself: are you a Hindu or a Muslim?"

Guru Jee replied, "My village is in the West. I just planted some seeds before I came here. There is no one home to water the fields. After seeing what you were doing, I thought I can get the water there whilst being here."

Hearing this, everyone started to laugh. Some even described Guru Jee as 'mad,' others said 'he is a simpleton'. One of the people said, "The water is not reaching your fields - it is just falling back into the water here."

Guru Jee said, "If my thrown water cannot reach my fields here on earth in Punjab, how will your thrown water be received by your ancestors millions of miles away, or reach the Sun? Please think about this."

Hearing this, they were all stunned into silence and started to think. One of them said, "He is saying the truth."

A second person said, "We were mistaken - his teaching is very good."

A third person said, "The Pandits (Hindu priests) have made fools of us, by getting us to follow their teachings."

Guru Jee then turned his attention to some Pandits who were meditating with rosaries. Guru Jee said, "Your thoughts are leading you to hell. Day and night, you are doing things for show and you are engaged in false practises. You have rosaries in your hands but your minds are engrossed in worldly affairs."

Guru Jee then said to one Pandit, "You are meditating but your mind is in Multan (a city)."

Guru Jee then said to another Pandit, "Your mind is in Kabul."

They said to another, "Your mind is in Delhi. You are thinking about what business will be the most profitable for you."

Guru Jee told them all what they were thinking. Hearing these words from Guru Jee, they all realised that Guru Jee is God incarnate. They said to Guru Jee, "We did not recognise you. Please forgive us. Make us your disciples (Sikhs)."

Guru Jee got them all to be seated and said, "The God that you meditate upon, believe that God to be present at all times and imbue this within your minds. Keep your mind on God at all times."

The Pandits got food ready. They requested Guru Jee to eat it. Guru Jee refused to go with them and to eat the food. The Pandits said, "Guru Jee, please come and eat the food."

Hearing this, Guru Jee went to their kitchen. The Khatris and Brahmins took their clothes off and sat down in the Square (a purified space called a Chownka). They washed Guru Jee's feet and got Them to sit in the Square, too, and they drew a line. Guru Jee said to them, "You have polluted the Square. Why are you drawing lines?"

The Brahmins said, "We have prepared the food with much purity (sucham). The Square is pasted with cow dung. No one else was allowed near the Square. The firewood was washed before use and all grain was washed prior to cooking it. We sat nearby and cooked the food with great purity. Why are you saying the kitchen has been polluted (in preparing the food)?"

Guru Jee said, "Until you hadn't arrived, the Square was pure - it got polluted with your arrival. The lowly have come with you."

The Pandits were confused and replied, "We cannot see anyone like this. Where are they? The kitchen is pure. Please eat the food. If you do not eat, then tell us who the lowly are that you see. Without telling us who they are, we cannot believe you."

Guru Jee then uttered the following Salok in Gurbani:

Corrupt intellect is the minstrel woman (mirasi caste); cruelty is the female butcher; slander of others in one's heart is the cleaning-woman (choori) and extreme anger and violence is the outcast-woman (chandalani). What good are the ceremonial lines drawn around your kitchen, when these four women of sin are seated there with you? (91 Ang)

Your corrupt intellect is a Mirasin (wife of a Mirasi). Your corrupt mercy (cruelty) is not reserved for all, therefore it is the butcher's wife. The slander of others that you do, is the cleaner in you. The demoness of violence in you is the wife of anger. All these four lowly women are looting you in your hearts. What purity is left by the drawing of lines to make your Square of purity? There is no purity as you are all polluted yourselves. These low caste women are sitting with you."

The Pandits asked, "How can the Square become purified now, then?"

Guru Jee then uttered these lines, continuing this Shabad:

"Make truth your self-discipline, make good deeds the lines you draw; make chanting God's name your cleansing bath. O Nanak, those who do not walk in the ways of sin, shall be exalted in the world hereafter. (91 Ang)

70

Make the Square pure by controlling your senses, stopping them from sinning, becoming free of corruption. Make lines (containing your self-discipline) by committing altruistic actions which are free of desires. Meditate on God's name - make that your purifying bathing. In the afterlife, those who refrains from sinful ways are honoured. In this way, the Square is purified and the dirt of the mind is removed."

Hearing Guru Jee's words, everyone started to contemplate their own demerits. They started to think: how can we rid ourselves of these bad characteristics? Now, they all supplicated to Guru Jee, "Please make us your Sikhs (disciples). We are in your sanctuary. Keep our honour and ferry us across the world ocean as you know how to. You are God incarnate."

Seeing their submission, Guru Jee said, "All the wealth you have, spend it all in God's name. Then we will make you our Sikhs."

Those who obeyed Guru Jee and spent all their money in this way were taught about God, inducted as Sikhs and obtained bliss of their souls (Atma).

At night, the River Ganga took on the form of a woman and came to Guru Jee. She had a tray of gold that was filled with pearls which she offered to Guru Jee as a gift. She bowed to Guru Jee and said, "Oh God, I cannot carry the burden of sins in Kaljug. Please bless me with a solution with which I can be at peace and in bliss (sukhi) always. You have taken on a human body to help others."

Guru Jee said to the River Ganga, "In the mornings and in the evenings, think of God's believers. When they put their blessed feet in your water, all the sins you are burdened with will be destroyed.'

71

Guru Jee also said, "This tray of jewels is of no use to us. Use it to feed Saints that are dedicated to God (to do a Bhandara – a feast for Saints)."

The River Ganga said, "Please bless me with your presence when the Bhandara is done. Please come and eat, too."

In the morning, after sunrise, the River Ganga organised her Bhandara. Many different dishes were prepared and all the angels (devte) were also invited. The angels came disguised as human beings. Guru Jee also went to it. Everyone bowed to Guru Jee. The food was prepared by the angels. Guru Jee washed the feet of all the Saints who arrived to eat in the Bhandara. When all the food had been served and eaten, all the angels came and bowed to Guru Jee and left. The River Ganga came and bowed to Guru Jee and went and became immersed in the River again.

People started asking one another, "Who organised this Bhandara?" Everyone was confused, as no name was given of who organised it.

Guru Jee stayed here for a few days. Whoever met Guru Jee was taught about being devoted to God.

Revision Questions Chapter 16

1) At Haridwar in the River, what were people doing and what did Guru Jee do?
2) How did Guru Jee teach the people that the water they were throwing was not reaching their ancestors?
3) What did Guru Jee say to those who were meditating with rosaries in their hands?
4) When the Pandits took Guru Jee to their square (chownkha) to eat, what did Guru Jee say?

72

5) When the River Ganga came to Guru Jee, what did she say and what did Guru Jee say?

Chapter 17
Guru Jee goes to Triaraj

Guru Jee now arrived at the kingdom of Noor Shah. Bhai Mardana asked Guru Jee, "Where can I go to drink water? I am thirsty." Guru Jee gave him permission to enter the city.

When he arrived in the city, he saw a woman in a doorway. Bhai Mardana asked her for drinking water. She replied, "Come inside and drink water." Bhai Mardana went inside and sat down to drink water. The woman asked Bhai Mardana, "From what country have you come from? Where are you travelling to?"

Bhai Mardana replied, "We are from Punjab. My name is Mardana. We are touring the world." The woman had only called Bhai Mardana inside to put a thread, with spells on it, over his neck! She did this now and Bhai Mardana became a sheep. She tied him to a post. She left with a water pitcher to fetch some water.

Guru Jee and Bhai Bala were sitting outside the city. Guru Jee knew what had happened and They now said, "Mardana has not returned. Hopefully he hasn't met misfortune like before."

Guru Jee got up and started to make Their way to the city. The woman was now returning with a full water pitcher. Guru Jee said to her, "A companion of ours came to drink water and he did not return to us."

She replied, "No companion of yours came this way - he must have gone in another direction."
Bhai Mardana was tied indoors so he was unable to do anything at this point. But he started to belch out like a sheep in the hope of getting Guru Jee's attention.

Guru Jee now said to the woman, "You are lying. Our companion is here."

The woman said, "If you do not believe me then go inside and have a look for yourselves."

Guru Jee made the water pitcher, which she was carrying, to become stuck on her head. She tried desperately to remove the pitcher from her head but she could not move it. Guru Jee said, "God is the wonderful enlightener," and the thread around Bhai Mardana's neck broke and he returned to his normal human body.

The women of the city were trying desperately to break or remove the water pitcher from the woman's head; their spells all failed and nothing they tried worked. The water pitcher was stuck on her had like unbreakable iron.

Noor Shah was the ruler here. She was told that a Saint with miraculous powers had arrived. She was told about the water pitcher on the woman's head and she got really angry. She sent all her experts in spells to have the water pitcher removed. One of the women arrived at the scene flying in on a wall, whilst another flew in on the deer's stable and another arrived playing a drum. None of them succeeded, no one could remove the pitcher from the woman's head.

The news was relayed to Noor Shah that all efforts they made failed to remove the pitcher. She now came herself. She wanted to see Guru Jee for herself. She tried many spells, too, but none worked. She failed, too, as did all her efforts. Nobody could remove the water pitcher from the woman's head.

The woman who had the water pitcher on her head was in much anguish. She was humbled and she realised she was wrong for lying to Guru Jee. She asked Noor Shah to seek forgiveness for her, from Guru Jee. Now, Noor Shah realised, too, that Guru Jee is the Saint of all Saints. Noor Shah fell at Guru Jee's feet and she begged Guru Jee in the following way: "I did not recognise your true nature. Please forgive me. Bless us by removing the pitcher from her head. You are the most powerful. No one is your equal."

Seeing them humbled, Guru Jee said, "Say 'God is the wonderful enlightener' and remove the pitcher off her head." In this way, the pitcher was removed from the woman's head. All the women were amazed by this and they all presented gifts and money to Guru Jee and said, "Oh perfect being, forgive us. Accept our offerings."

Hearing their pleas, Guru Jee blessed them with words of advice. The women were filled with the emotion of detachment (bairaag) in their hearts. The women said, "Forgive us. For the betterment of mankind, you are travelling the globe. We now know your greatness. Bless us with your teachings and accept our offerings. We have wasted our lives up until this point."

When Guru Jee heard their words of submission, Guru Jee blessed them with Amrit from their feet (charan pahul) and made them Sikhs. Guru Jee got them to build a Dharamsala and got them to do daily sadh-sangat (holy congregation). Guru Jee advised them, "Meditate on the wonderous enlightener God at all times. God will destroy all anguish from your lives. Whoever comes here, do not use spells on them. Instead, serve any visitors as guests."

Guru Jee stayed here for a while. After teaching the women about love and devotional practises, Guru Jee travelled on.

Revision Questions Chapter 17

1) When Bhai Mardana went to drink water, what happened?

2) When the woman lied to Guru Jee what happened? What did Guru Jee do?

3) How was the water pitcher removed from her head?

4) What teachings did Guru Jee give these women?

Chapter 18
Kagh Bhasund

Blessing the North Himalayan range of mountains and surrounding areas, Guru Jee visited Nepal, Bhutan, Tibet, China, Mansarovar Cheel, Kailash mountain and Sumer mountain – where They did the Sidha Goshat discussion with Yogis. They also met Kagh Bhasund ('Kagh' means crow, 'Bhasund' was his name) after meeting the Yogis upon their descent from these mountains. This crow is the most respected bird and many birds live with him. He teaches the other birds about God, devotedly narrating discourses about God. The location of where Kagh Bhasund lives is said to be on the ascent to Hemkunt Sahib on a section of the mountains which is not accessible by man. A sign can be seen on the path when climbing up, which points out the direction in which he is believed to reside.

Whilst Kagh Bhasund was giving one of his discourses, Guru Jee, Bhai Bala and Bhai Mardana went and sat there. When the discourse ended, all of the birds bowed to him. After this, Bhai Mardana did kirtan, during which Kagh Bhasund fell into a deep meditative state. After finishing the Shabad (hymn), Bhai Mardana went silent and remained seated there. Kagh Bhasund opened his eyes and lovingly asked Bhai Mardana, "Who has authored these hymns? This hymn burns worldly attachment, which is like a jungle. I have been drenched in love listening to it. Tell me the name of the author of this hymn. The author must be extremely devout and imbued in the colour of devotion."

Bhai Mardana said, "This Shabad is uttered by Sri Guru Nanak Dev Jee. They are the incarnation of the all-pervasive God." Hearing this, Kagh Bhasund bowed at Guru Jee's feet. Seeing this, all of the other birds also bowed at Guru Jee's feet. Kagh Bhasund said, "I had received this news earlier that God had taken incarnation in Kaljug. I desired to have your blessed sight (Darshan). You knew this and came to bless me, so you have fulfilled my desire. You have come to put sinners on the correct path of devotion to God. Those who take your sanctuary will be freed from the cycle of births and deaths. Your hymns have the power and wisdom to do this. Reading these hymns, people in kaljug (present era of sin) will definitely attain liberation."

Guru Jee said to Kagh Bhasund, "You are great in all virtues and you single-mindedly imbue yourself in devotion. You are the greatest listener."

Kagh Bhasund said, "You are the master of the meek - tell me, how many types of listeners are there?"

Guru Jee said, "There are five types of listeners. Firstly, who understands the Raag (musical tune); secondly, those who understand the notes; thirdly, those who understand the beat, fourthly, those who listen to music and fifthly, those who understand the hymn – who are supreme. The other four types of listeners only realise the 'skin' (outer superficial level) and not the inner meaning. You have enjoyed the bliss of Sadh-Sangat (congregation of the holy) and have obtained a very, very long life."

Bhai Bala asked, "Oh Saint, please tell us your age. How many ages have passed during your lifetime?"

Kagh Bhasund said, "My age is beyond example or counting. When 100 ages (jugs) pass, it is one night of Brahma (the angel of creation) and a further 100 ages (jug) pass for a day of his. I have seen many Brahmas die, who each die after 100 years. I have seen destruction many times of the whole world and then a new Brahma starts to create the world again. I sit here singing God's praises."

Bhai Bala said, "You are a great devotee (Bhagat) of God. You have destroyed your attachment to the world and have attained wisdom of your soul (Atma-Gian). You are great. How did you get the body of a crow?"

Kagh Bhasund replied, "I will now narrate how I became a crow so listen carefully. In one birth, I was born into a low-caste family. I was devoted to Shiva Jee (angel of destruction) and served him (did seva) and I was opposed to Vishnu Jee (angel of sustenance). I lived in Ayodhya. A disease broke out there, a contagious one. I left there and went to Ujjain. There was a true Saint there, who knew the essence of God and had realised God. He was called Manchain (meaning he whose mind is at rest or peaceful). I took him on as my Guru. He taught me to become devoted to Vishnu Jee. I used to burn in hatred, when I used to hear the praise of Vishnu Jee. I was still devoted to Shiva Jee. Out of stubbornness, I used to refuse the instructions of my Guru on many occasions, in light of my dislike of Vishnu Jee. I did not want to hear these words of instruction but my Guru still continued to attempt to teach me in many different ways. But I still would not listen. I was stuck in my ego and false devotion.

One day, I was seated in Shiva Jee's temple. My merciful Guru also arrived there. I did not rise upon his entrance, thus I disrespected him nor did I bow to him. I sat there in ego. My Guru was a knower of God. They saw respect, disrespect, happiness, sadness, all in the same way – equally. They still did not curse me after my disrespect. Out of the temple, a voice was heard which said, "Oh tyrant go to hell now. Then go enter lowly lifeforms. Reap the fruit of sin for disrespecting your Guru. You are false and egotistical. You daily oppose Vishnu Jee and disrespect your Guru. For this reason, now receive punishment from deaths messengers."

When my Guru heard this curse, he became merciful. He supplicated to Shiva Jee in many ways. Then Shiva Jee spoke and said, "Oh Brahman, due to your mercy, he will remember all his lives which he is to undergo. My curse will remain, in hell he will suffer a lot."

Kagh Bashund said, "Then I fell into hells. The death messengers (jamdhoot) made me suffer a lot. After a long time in these hells, I was freed. Then, I was reborn into all the 8.4 million lives. I underwent every single life form and I prayed to God in creation (doing Sargun Upasna). I remembered all my pervious lives, Shiva Jee's curse and boon turned out to be true.

One day Lomas Rikhi (a famous Saint with a very long age) came by and I sat down to listen to their words. They taught me to pray to God without form (do Nirgun Upasna). I had no inclination in my heart for devotion with this method. They taught me in many ways how to do this. I continually asked about Sargun Upasna and kept on raising doubts about Nirgun Upasna. Seeing my opposing nature, Lomas Rikhi spoke in anger to me saying, "Your words are of questioning. You continually refuse my advice. I was teaching you, thinking you are worthy of this advice, now become a crow, as you continually prattle like one, undergo this curse."

I then took up the body of a crow. I praised Lomas Rikhi, clasped my hands and said, "Rikhi Jee, your words have become true. Know me to be your slave, please bless me and be merciful. Bless me that I still maintain knowledge, even if I am in the body of a crow."

Hearing this Lomas, Rikhi said, "You will maintain knowledge in your mind. I have now blessed you. I grant you a boon – you will only die, when you desire it."

Hearing these words, I then came and started living here. My mind is now at peace. I do not feel like leaving this body, I have imbued loving devotion (Bhagti) to God in this body of a crow. I am in bliss at all times."

In this way, Kagh Bhasund narrated his history. Guru Jee then left.

Revision Questions Chapter 18

1. Which route did Guru Jee take to get to Kagh Bhasund?
2. When Kagh Bhasund heard Bhai Mardana Jee sing the shabad what did he ask?
3. How many types of listeners did Guru Jee describe? Also, what were these types?
4. What age did Kagh Bhasund say he was?
5. In his previous life how did Kagh Bhasund disrespect his Guru?
6. Why did Lomas curse Kagh Bhasund?

Chapter 19
Dhru Bhagat

From the Sumer Mountain, Guru Jee went on to meet Bhagat Prehlad, Datta Dhre and others, and then arrived at Dhru's planet. On the way to this planet, Bhai Mardana asked, "Guru Jee, stars are not seen here."

Guru Jee said, "The stars are now below where we are. Dhru's planet (the Northern Star) is above us. The light from Dhru's planet is giving us light here. He became devoted to God at a young age and performed great penance (as meditation) and got the highest star as his home."

Bhai Mardana said, "Please narrate Dhru's history to us, of how he achieved an eternal kingdom upon his planet and allow us to see that planet, too."

Guru Jee said, "In Satjug (age of truth which occurred thousands of years ago) there was a king called Uttaanpad. He had two queens called Sruchi and Suneeta. The king favoured Sruchi. Dhru was the first-born and Suneeta was his mother. Sruchi's son, Uttam, was born afterwards. Once, when Dhru was five years, old he went to his father, Uttaanpad. His father lovingly met him and sat him upon his lap. Seeing this, Sruchi was angered and grabbed Dhru by the arm. She removed him from his father's lap. She wanted her son to be crowned king and did not want Dhru to get close to his father. Sruchi said to Dhru, "If you desire the throne then die and be reborn to me." Seeing all this, the king did not say anything.

Crying, Dhru went to his mother and was very hurt and angry. He told his mother what had happened. Dhru's mother was very upset hearing about Sruchi's behaviour. She sat Dhru in her laps and said, "Oh son, anguish and pleasure are the fruits of our actions. From previous good actions, we get pleasure and from previous bad actions, we get anguish. I am a queen, but in my previous life I did no bhagti (devotion to God). For this reason, I am not even treated as fairly as a slave girl (many slave girls were attendants in kingdoms then). If you desire the kingdom then single-mindedly meditate upon God. Your grandfather (paternal) Manu, performed many yags (sacrificial ceremonies) and obtained pleasure by meditating upon God." Hearing this teaching, Dhru bowed to his mother and left to meditate in the jungle. On the way, he met Narad Muni (a famous saint who is the son of Brahma). Narad blessed Dhru by putting his hand upon his head and said, "Oh son, upon hearing your step-mother's words, you have come to the jungle. You are but a child, who should enjoy eating, drinking and playing. You should not contemplate happiness and sadness, or why it occurs. Doing such penance of meditation is not right. Go home to live there. There is no pleasure in the jungle, there are many wild beasts in the jungle. They will make you suffer. If you meditate for a long time and try many methods, you still will not attain God. When you enter your youth then do this."

Hearing Narad Muni's words, Dhru clasped his hands and said, "I am a bad person! Hearing my step-mother's words, my chest is burning. You live for altruism at all times. The stage that my grandfather did not even reach - I want to attain that."

Hearing these words of faith from Dhru, Narad Muni was elated and said, "I was testing you. The path of liberation that your mother has taught you is correct. Go to the jungle and meditate upon Vishnu. I will give you Gurmantar (words invested into a disciple from their Guru). You meditate upon this Gurmantar, with single minded concentration then you will obtain whatever you desire." In this way, Narad Muni imparted Gurmantar to Dhru. Dhru bowed to Narad Muni and went deeper into the jungle.

Narad Muni then went to the king. The king was depressed after being separated from his son, Dhru. Narad Muni was seated respectfully by the king and the king bowed to him. Narad Muni said, "Oh king, why is your forehead full of stress and what wrong has taken place?"

The king said, "Oh great saint, I am ignorant. I relinquished my five year old son, who has no fault of his own. He has gone to the jungle to perform meditative penance (tap). In the jungle, he will suffer from hunger, thirst and a host of difficulties and pain. How will he endure all this?"

Narad Muni said, "Oh king, do not worry about your son as God is all pervading. He is engrossed in God's meditation and he will come back to you in a short time. He will be praised all over the world upon his return." Saying this, Narad Muni left.

Dhru started doing very difficult penance: after every three days, he would eat some fruits from the jungle. He passed the first month like this. In the second month, he started eating only grass. In the third month, he ate dry leaves and drank water only. In the fourth month, he ate every twelve days. In the fifth month, he survived only on air and stood on one foot whilst meditating. When he did such stringent penance, even the earth started to waiver and people got scared. The angels went to Vishnu and said, "Oh beloved, all beings are in anguish - remove this anguish."

Vishnu said, "Do not get scared, my children. My devotee is performing a great penance. I will now go to him." The angels left after hearing this. Dhru was meditating upon Vishnu in his heart. Vishnu broke Dhru's concentration with his powers and Dhru opened his eyes. He now saw the same Vishnu he was meditating upon in front of him. Dhru tried to praise Vishnu but he was powerless to do so. Vishnu knew

Dhru's desire, thus he put his conch on Dhru's lips and pulled away. This infused the power to sing Vishnu's praises inside of him and he then praised him profusely. Then he bowed upon Vishnu's feet. Seeing all this, Vishnu was pleased and he said, "Oh prince, I know all your desires. Now, take up your seat on the highest platform that no one else has ever attained. You will now rule as the king for 36,000 years, after which you will get the highest kingdom. Your step-brother, Uttam, is forever wanting to go hunting. He will go to war against the angels (devte) in the jungle. The angels will kill him. Your step-mother will then go searching for him in the jungle. She will die in a fire in the jungle. The whole kingdom is yours now. Now go home - your mother and father are awaiting your return." After saying this, Vishnu disappeared.

After getting these boons, Dhru returned home. The king was elated when he learnt of the return of his son. The person who gave him this news was showered with gifts. The king got musicians to play and he went forward with them and his two queens, to welcome Dhru back. His step brother and many others, also came along. When the king saw Dhru, he dismounted from his chariot and lovingly embraced Dhru. Uttam also happily greeted his brother. Dhru bowed at the feet of his father. His father put his hand on his head and blessed him. They all returned to the palace and the festivities followed, celebrating Dhru's return. The king seeing his own old age, crowned Dhru the next king. The king now left the palace to go and perform penance and meditations in the jungle. Dhru was married to a woman called Prami. She had two sons with Dhru called Vastar and Kalpank.

Uttam went to the jungle to hunt and got into a battle with Jashs (angels who are servants of Kuber) and Uttam was killed. His mother went in search of him and also died from a jungle fire (bush fire). When Dhru learnt of his brother's death, he declared war against the Jashs and went and fought against them, killing many of them.

Dhru's paternal grandfather, Manu, became merciful upon the Jashs and he came to Dhru and said, "Do not kill the innocent Jashs. You are God's devotee so have mercy. They killed one brother of yours but you have killed countless numbers of their army. Now stop fighting." Dhru now stopped fighting and Manu returned to his home.

Now, Kuber came and said to Dhru, "Oh king, you are great. You obeyed your grandfather. You have relinquished anger from your mind. The Jashs did not kill your brother, nor did you kill any Jashs. The killer of all is kaal (death and time). You did great penance and meditation as a child. I am happy with you. Whatever boon you desire, I will grant it to you."

Dhru replied, "Bless me with the boon that I have eternal devotion and love for the feet of God."

Kuber replied "So be it." Kuber then left. Dhru returned to his own kingdom.

Dhru ruled for 36,000 years and then gave the crown to his son. Dhru went and sat at the riverbanks of the Ganga and performed penance and meditation. An astral vehicle appeared near him. The Gans (servants of angels) bowed to Dhru (they had brought the vehicle down) and they said, "It is God's command that you be seated upon this vehicle, to be taken to your eternal kingdom."

Hearing this, Dhru bathed in the river Ganga and sat in the vehicle. The angels now showered Dhru with flowers and music bellowed out and praise of Dhru was heard. Dhru went to the highest star, which was to be his planet – the Northern Star.

After narrating this history of Dhru to Bhai Mardana, Guru Jee also went to Dhru's planet.

When Guru Jee arrived, Dhru was walking. When he saw Guru Jee, he enquired, "With which power have these three men arrived here?"

When Guru Jee went near Dhru, They said, "The Creator God is eternal."

Dhru enquired, "You live an earth. How did you travel here and who are you? Where will you travel to next? No-one has come here before in human form."

Guru Jee said, "With the power of devotion to the creator God, we have travelled here on our way to have blessed sight (darshan) of the all-pervasive God. You meditated on God a lot as a child. My name is Nanak."

When Dhru heard Guru Jee's name, he clasped his hands and bowed at Guru Jee's feet and said, "I had received news earlier that God had taken incarnation on earth. You have blessed me by coming to give me darshan." In this way, a conversation took place. Guru Jee stayed here for a little while then travelled on to Sachkand, whilst leaving Bhai Bala and Bhai Mardana on Dhru's planet.

Revision Questions Chapter 19

1. Where did Guru Jee travel to on the way to Dhrus planet?

2. What did Dhru's step-mother say to him when she removed him from his father's lap?

3. When Dhru came home crying what did his mother instruct him to do?

4. For how long and in what ways did Dhru perform mediations and penance in the jungle?

5. Why did Dhru kill the Jash's in battle and who stopped him fighting more?

6. For how long did Dhru rule for on earth? After this where did he go?

Chapter 20
Sajjan Thag

Sri Guru Nanak Dev Jee now left Rai Bhue Dee Talvandi (Nankana Sahib) with the son of Bhai Mardana, Shehzada, and Bhai Bala, as Bhai Mardana had now passed away. Guru Jee was now taking Shehzada to the site of cremation of Bhai Mardana (which is in an Iranian cemetery near the Khorrum River and in Khorrumshaer). On the journey there, they came to a place called Tulumba. Tulumba village is now in the district of Multan in Pakistan. Here lived a thief called Sajjan. He had made a Dharamsala here. Upon entry into this Dharamsala, he built a mosque on one side and a temple on another side and an accommodation block for people to stay in. He wore the attire of that of saints. He took up this dress to defraud people and thieve off them. If any traveller came to this place, he would serve them immensely first by giving them good food and a bed to rest. Afterwards, he and his companions would then murder the guests and steal all their belongings.

Guru Jee came and sat down near Tulumba Village. Shehzada got hungry. He got permission from Guru Jee to enter the village to eat there. He saw the Dharamsala – he entered it and greeted Sajjan. Sajjan spoke to him with respect and said, "Come brother, where have you come from? What is your name? What is your caste?" Shehzada sat down near Sajjan and said, "My name is Shehzada, I am a mirasi (minstrel) by caste and we are very far from our homes. I have come here to eat food."

Sajjan replied, "We have plenty of food. Who is your master and whose mirasi are you? Is he greater than me?"

Shehzada said, "My beloved is a lot greater than you. Whatever you ask off him, you obtain. He is a Khatri by caste (warrior caste) and his name is Nanak."

Sajjan now said to his servant, "He is the mirasi of a great man. Serve him well."

The servant now took Shehzda inside to eat. Three men then appeared. They captured Shehzada, tied him up and stripped him off his belongings and clothes. Then, they started to beat him up, whilst also asking, "Tell us if you have any other belongings or we will kill you immediately."
Shehzada was in severe pain and started to remember Guru Jee and started to think, 'Guru Jee, look where you sent me to eat! I am in much pain now. I mistakenly took him for a saint. I did not know he is a sinner!'

When Shehzada mentally called out for Guru Jee to save him, Guru Jee then set off to rescue him. Upon arrival, Guru Jee said, "God is the supreme creator, God is the supreme creator."

Guru Jee now asked Sajjan, "Our mirasi came to eat food here but he has not returned to us."

Sajjan said, "You look like a great saint, therefore, I cannot lie in front of you. If you don't trust me then have a look." (Sajjan pointed at a room).

Guru Jee said to Bhai Bala, "Bring Shehzada out from inside and blacken his face (referring to Sajjan)."

Bhai Bala quickly went inside. Shehzada was tied up with ropes. Bhai Bala untied him and brought him out.

Guru Jee asked, "Why are you naked? Who took your clothes?"

Shehzada replied, "You sent me to a great place to eat! They even stripped me off my clothes. Get my clothes back off them. They are tyrants and sinners!"

The men there replied, "He arrived here naked."

Shehzada said, "He dresses like a good saint but there is no other evil sinner like him. They held me inside, stripped me naked and tied me up with ropes and beat me. They repeatedly asked if I had more money or possessions, threatening to kill me if I did not tell them."

As Shehzada narrated what had happened, Sajjan was becoming more and more ashamed, lowering his neck. Sajjan had no answers. He had nowhere to hide either. Guru Jee then instructed Sajjan in the following way, "Oh Sajjan, you have an outwardly dress of saints but internally you are a sinner. At your end, when you die, who will then free you when death's messengers come to punish you? The money of sin that you have accumulated will then be of no assistance to you. Those for whom you collate this money, cannot save you from punishment in the afterlife nor will they be of any help then. You will then go into hells, suffer and regret what you did."

Hearing these fearful words, Sajjan fell at the feet of Guru Jee and said, "Maharaj Jee, I have committed many sins - please bless and forgive me. I am in your sanctuary. Your nature is altruistic. Hearing your words, I have realised all this."

Guru Jee said, "If you agree to not sin again then God will forgive you."

Sajjan said, "Maharaj Jee, I will never sin again. Forgive my previous sins, bless me with your teachings and make me your Sikh. Seeing my evil actions, you purposely came here to bless me." Sajjan now fell at Guru Jee's feet again.

Guru Jee said, "Meditate on God's true name at all times, with which you will be bettered. Take this Mirasi on as your Guru."

Accepting Guru Jee's advice, Sajjan then fell at Shehzada's feet.

Guru Jee said, "All the money you have amassed through sins, give it all out to the poor."

Sajjan accepted Guru Jee's advice and distributed all of his wealth to the poor. In this way, Sajjan was reformed and Guru Jee travelled onwards from here.

Revision Questions Chapter 20

1) What sort of dress was Sajjan wearing and what sort of person was he?
2) When Shehzada went to Sajjan, what did Sajjan say and how was Shehzada treated afterwards?
3) What teachings did Guru Jee give to Sajjan?
4) What did Guru Jee instruct Sajjan to do in terms of taking on a Guru?

Chapter 21
Sri Lehna Jee

In the district of Amritsar is a very old village called Khadur. During the times of Sri Guru Nanak Dev Jee, a saintly person called Lehna lived there. His paternal village was 2km from Mukhtsar Sahib and is called Matte dee Sarai. Raiders from Baloch looted and destroyed the village. After this happened, Sri Lehna Jee started living at Khadur.

Sri Lehna Jee's soul took up the embodiment of a human form on 15th March 1504 CE. He was born in Nange Dee Sarai village to father Phiru Mal and mother Deya Kaur (Sabhrayee) Jee. His wife Mata Khivi Jee was from Khadur. His father in law was Devi Das and mother in law Bhirayee Jee - they were from the village Sangher which is 4km from Kahdur Sahib, too.

Sri Lehna Jee had two sons: Dasu Jee and Datu Jee and two daughters, Bibi Amro Jee and Bibi Anokhi Jee. Sri Lehna Jee used to pray to an angel (Devi). Annually, along with others, they would lead congregations to Jawalamukhi in Kangra to visit shrines of the Devi. In Khadur Sahib, there lived a Sikh called Bhai Jodha Jee. He did not believe or have faith in any others apart from Sri Guru Nanak Dev Jee. Daily, he would rise before dawn (Amrit Vela), bathe (do ishnaan) and recite Gurbani. One day, Sri Lehna Jee was passing by. He experienced much bliss when hearing Bhai Jodha read Gurbani. He asked Bhai Jodha, "The scriptures you are reading - who is the great soul who authored it? Where do they live?"

Bhai Jodha replied, "These words are those of Sri Guru Nanak Dev Jee - They live in Kartarpur."

Sri Lehna Jee got Bhai Jodha to write out some of these Shabads (verses) for him. Sri Lehna Jee thought, 'I will take on the author of these peace giving words as my Guru. I had already heard of their glorious praise from others. The time for the annual trip to Jawalamukhi is upon us; I will go to Kartarpur on my way there.'

The day to depart arrived and Sri Lehna Jee addressed the group of devotees who were about to depart, "Let's go via Kartarpur. We can have the blessed sight (darshan) of Sri Guru Nanak Dev Jee there."

Everyone agreed with this suggestion. They travelled and arrived at Kartarpur and asked a man upon arrival, "Whose village is this?"

Then man replied, "This is the village of the great spiritualist, Sri Guru Nanak Dev Jee. People come from far to congregate and seek guidance."

Sri Lehna said to his travelling group, "You all wait here. Let me go and get darshan (blessed sight) of Sri Guru Nanak Dev Jee."

Guru Jee thought: 'Our disciple, who is going to become the next Guru, is on his way.'

Guru Jee got up and came outside the village and stood on the road that Sri Lehna was going to travel on. Sri Lehna saw Guru Jee standing there and said, "I have come to get darshan of Sri Guru Nanak Dev Jee."

Guru Jee said to him, "Come with me and I will get you Their darshan."

In this way, Guru Jee walked ahead, whilst Sri Lehna Jee followed on his mare. When they arrived near the

Dharamsala, Guru Jee said to Sri Lehna, "Tie the mare here, go into that door ahead and do darshan." Guru Jee entered through another door and went and sat down.

Sri Lehna tied the mare and went inside and bowed to Guru Jee and thought, 'This is the same person who met me and brought me here.' He thought, 'I have made a grave mistake. If I knew who They were, then I would have got off the mare and bowed at their feet there and then. How will I now be forgiven?'

Guru Jee knew what Sri Lehna was thinking and asked, "What is your name and where are you from?"

Sri Lehna replied, "My name is Lehna. I live at Khadur. Hearing your praise, I longed for your darshan for some time. You have fulfilled this longing today."

Guru Jee said, "Those who are going to receive (meaning Lehna) they come seated upon a mare. Those who are going to give, they come by walking."

At this point, Sri Lehna thought, 'If they are the knower of hearts (antarjami) then they should tell me to go home. Then I will go home and come back.' At that moment, the all-knowing Guru Jee said, "Go home now and then return."

Sri Lehna Jee then believed in Guru Jee as his Guru, from thereon. Sri Lehna bowed at Guru Jee's feet and left. When he arrived back to his travelling group, he said to them, "You go on to Jawalamukhi. I am going back to Khadur." They parted ways there.

Sri Lehna arrived at Khadur. People in his village asked, "Why did you not go to Jawalamukhi?"

Sri Lehna Jee did not answer these questions. He came straight home. He arose at Amrit Vela and packed 1.25 ser (approximately 50kg) in salt and set off carrying this to Kartarpur. He arrived at Kartarpur and deposited the salt safely there (donating it) and asked Mata Sulakhni (wife of Sri Guru Nanak Dev Jee), "Where is Guru Jee?"

She replied, "They have gone to the fields to get their disciples to do some work."

Sri Lehna Jee then set off to meet Guru Jee in the fields. Guru Jee was getting the Sikhs to pull grass and weeds from the field of rice. Sri Lehna Jee bowed at Guru Jee's feet and started to do this work, too. When some time passed, Guru Jee said, "You are not doing this work correctly. This grass that has been pulled out, tie it up and take it back to feed the cattle."

Sri Lehna Jee packed the grass into a pile and tied it all together and carried it back as instructed. Dirt and debris fell from the grass he was carrying and his silk clothes got stained and ruined. He did not pay any attention to this. He fed the grass to the cattle. Seeing this, Mata Sulakhni Jee was shocked and said, "All his clothes and head is covered in mud."

When Guru Jee arrived back with his disciples from the fields, Mata Sulakhni Jee said, "The pious man, who arrived today, has ruined his expensive clothes and is covered from head to toe in mud."

Guru Jee said, "This pile of grass that he carried upon his head is giving him the crown of ruling the whole world. What you see as mud is us spraying saffron upon him."

When Guru Jee said this, all the mud and stains now turned into saffron. Mata Jee said, "Only you know your ways."

Guru Jee said, "He will become the boatman to ferry across those drowning in sin in kaljug (the present era of sin)."

Revision Questions Chapter 21

1) What was the name of the original village (paternal) of Sri Lehna Jee? What were the names of his mother and father?

2) Where is Jawalamukhi?

3) Who did Sri Lehna hear reciting Gurbani, which led to him wanting to take on Sri Guru Nanak Dev Jee as his Guru?

4) What did Guru Jee say to Sri Lehna about how those who are to take and the way in which they arrive? What did they say about those who are to give, go to them?

5) What did Guru Jee say to Mata Sulakhni about Sri Lehna's muddy clothes and what it all meant?

Chapter 22
Sri Guru Angad Dev Jee

A lot of saints started coming to Kartarpur to get darshan of Sri Guru Nanak Dev Jee. For this reason, there was always a lot of temporary accommodation erected all around the village to house these guests. Guru Jee's Langar would run unabated.

A time came when it would not stop raining – it rained continuously for two days, therefore, Langar was not prepared (due to everything being wet). Seeing the people hungry, Guru Jee said to his eldest son, Baba Sri Chand, "That tree, which is there, go and shake it. Then a multitude of foods, desserts and dishes will fall from it. The people who are hungry can then eat."

Baba Sri Chand said, "I have never seen such foods growing on trees, nor heard of them. What are you talking of? If I do as you say, I will look silly and get shamed by people. For this reason, I will not climb the tree and shake it."

Then Guru Jee turned to his younger son, Lakhmi Das and said, "Son, climb the tree, shake it and get food for the hungry people." Lakhmi Das also refused to do this like his brother.

Then Guru Jee said to Sri Lehna, "You do this task. People are hungry."

Hearing Guru Jee's command, Sri Lehna Jee took the congregation along with him and got them to sit under the tree. He climbed the tree and shook it as hard as he could. Out of the tree numerous foods fell, such as desserts and meals, but nothing could be seen growing or hanging on the tree. The congregation ate these foods to their full then everyone returned and bowed at Guru Jee's feet.

Guru Jee would daily go to the River Ravi to do Ishnaan before sunrise. Sri Lehna Jee would go with Them and hold Their clothes on the riverbank. Once, it was winter and it was raining, Sri Lehna Jee fainted due to the exposure to the cold and rain. Guru Jee came out of the river immediately and put Their foot on Sri Lehna Jee's forehead and he came back around to being conscious. Guru Jee asked, "What happened?" Sri Lehna Jee replied, "Maharaj, the cold made me fall unconscious - now the blessed dust of Your feet has made me regain consciousness."

One night, Guru Jee said to his eldest son, Baba Sri Chand Jee, "Son, wash and dry this sheet at the river."

Baba Sri Chand Jee replied, "I am resting. My hands will freeze in the cold water. When the sun rises, we will get someone to wash the sheet."

Then, Guru Jee asked Baba Lakhmi Das Jee to wash the sheet; he also gave a similar reply and refused to do it.

Guru Jee asked Sri Lehna Jee, "Go and wash our sheet and dry it." He left immediately to wash the sheet at the river. When he arrived there, he saw the afternoon sun. He washed the sheet, dried it and returned. When he arrived back, it was night there.

One night, Guru Jee threw a bowl into a ditch. Guru Jee said to Baba Sri Chand Jee, "Son, our bowl has fallen into the dirty ditch. Take it out and clean it." Baba Sri Chand Jee replied, "My clothes will get dirty in the mud. Tell a Sikh to get it out."

Then Guru Jee said to Baba Lakhmi Das Jee, "Get the dish."

He replied, "Father, you are very wise as you get us to do the dirty tasks. I will never do this dirty work."

Guru Jee said to Sri Lehna Jee, "Go and fetch the bowl."

When Sri Lehna Jee heard this command of the Guru, he immediately jumped into the ditch and fetched the bowl. He then washed it thoroughly and presented it to Guru Jee. Sri Lehna Jee's clothes, from head to toe, were covered in mud. Seeing this, everyone was shocked and started to say, "He is great."

On one occasion, Baba Buddha Jee thought, 'I serve Guru Jee and obey them too. I am not sure why Guru Jee blesses Sri Lehna Jee so much?' Guru Jee knew Baba Buddha Jee's thoughts and wanted to now test his faith. So, at night Guru Jee said, "Buddha, go out and have a look at how much nightfall is remaining. Is it time to do Ishnaan or not?"

Baba Buddha Jee went out and looked and said, "Half the night is left."

Guru Jee said, "No, there is not that much left of it, only three hours remain." Guru Jee then said to Baba Buddha Jee, "Have a look properly and tell me."

Baba Buddha Jee assessed it again carefully and said, "Yes, half the night remains."

Guru Jee then, the third time, said again, "Look at how much nightfall remains."

Baba Buddha Jee again said, "Half the night remains."

Guru Jee said to Sri Lehna Jee, "Have a look at how much of the night remains. Sri Lehna Jee looked at the movement of the stars and approximated that half the night remained.

Guru Jee then said, "Look carefully – only three hours remain."

Sri Lehna Jee went outside again and looked carefully at the night sky. He thought: 'half the night is remaining (six hours), but who knows what is acceptable to Guru Jee? Only They know Their ways.' After thinking this, Sri Lehna Jee said to Guru Jee, "Maharaj, my eyes are full of sleep so, I mistakenly said half of the night remains. Whatever amount of night you have allocated to pass has passed; whatever remains of the night is also under your command."

Then Baba Buddha Jee understood that he could not follow Guru Jee's ways in the way that Sri Lehna Jee did. He now understood why Guru Jee was happy with him and favoured him.

One night, there was torrential rain and a wall collapsed in the rain. Guru Jee told his sons, "Go and repair the wall."

His sons replied, "You have many Sikhs who can do this."

Guru Jee said to the Sikhs, "Repair the wall."

The Sikhs said, "Yes, Guru Jee, let day break and the rain to stop then we will do it."

Guru Jee told Sri Lehna Jee to repair the wall. He said, "True word," and started reconstructing the wall. The wet wall kept collapsing but he kept rebuilding it. Sri Lehna Jee continued and thought, 'If it gets built or completed that is in the hands of the Guru.'

Afterwards, Guru Jee started to test the Sikhs further. Guru Jee tied a Langota (a loin cloth) around Their waist with a knife attached to it and gathered some dogs to accompany him. Sri Lehna Jee said to the Sikhs, "Don't be afraid as They are testing us."

When Guru Jee left for a walk dressed like this, many Sikhs accompanied Them. Guru Jee said, "Leave." When they didn't listen, Guru Jee, with His power, produced gold and silver coins that He piled up and said to the Sikhs, "Take these coins and go home." Some Sikhs left like this.

Those who remained said to Guru Jee, "We are your Sikhs - wherever you keep us, we will remain."

Guru Jee now started to hit everyone with a stick. When the Sikhs took a good beating, most of them ran back home. The few that remained were asked by Guru Jee, "What are you doing here? Why do you not leave?"

The Sikhs replied, "We are your Sikhs so we will remain with you."

Guru Jee asked, "How long have you been Sikhs?"

The Sikhs replied, "Since you made us your Sikhs."

Guru Jee said, "If you are my Sikhs then follow me."

Guru Jee now walked into the countryside and the Sikhs followed. Guru Jee now made a dead body appear there. A white sheet was spread over the body. Guru Jee now said, "If you are my Sikhs then eat this dead body - if you do not, you will regret it."

When the Sikhs heard these words they were shocked. Many great Sikhs, like Baba Buddha Jee, went out of sight, hiding behind trees, and some returned home. Only Sri Lehna Jee remained with Guru Jee. Guru Jee said to him, "Why are you standing here? Why have you not left?"

Sri Lehna Jee replied, "I am your Sikh. You can beat me but I will not leave your side."

Guru Jee said, "If you are not going to leave then eat this dead body."

Sri Lehna Jee started to walk around the dead body. Guru Jee asked, "Why are you not eating it? Why are you taking so long?"

Sri Lehna Jee said, "I was awaiting your command: from which side shall I start to eat?"

Guru Jee said, "Starting from the feet to the head - eat it all."

When Sri Lehna Jee lifted the sheet, there was Karah Parshad (a sweet sacrament given out at Gurdwaras, made up of flour, ghee, sugar and water) lying there in the form of a body. Sri Lehna Jee was astounded when he witnessed this and fell at Guru Jee's feet. He said, "You are all powerful! You are the incarnation of God." After some time, that parshad also disappeared.

Hearing these words from Sri Lehna Jee, Guru Jee was pleased and taught Sri Lehna Jee about divine wisdom and said, "Now you have become our form. There is no difference between us." In this way, Guru Jee proved to everyone how Sri Lehna Jee passed all Their tests and His perfection to be the next Guru.

After a few days, Guru Jee called everyone to the Dharamsala to make an announcement. Guru Jee placed five Paise (five coins of currency), a coconut in front of Sri Lehna Jee and did three Parkarma (circumambulations) around him and bowed at his feet, thus anointing him the next Guru.

Guru Jee said to Sri Lehna Jee, "From today, you are everyone's Guru. The world is your servant. By joining you to Our limbs, we have made you like ourselves. From this day onwards, you will be known as Sri Angad ('ang' means 'limb' - Sri Lehna became a limb of the Guru)."

Guru Jee told all those who had gathered, "All bow to him."

Everyone bowed to Sri Guru Angad Dev Jee but Guru Jee's sons did not. Guru Jee now said to Sri Guru Angad Dev Ji, "Now, leave here and go to your own village. My sons will make life hard for you due to their jealousy. Obeying Guru Jee, Sri Guru Angad Dev Jee departed for Khadur Sahib."

Revision Questions Chapter 22

1) When it didn't stop raining for two days what did Guru Jee say to his sons? Who completed the task in the end?

2) What did Guru Jee tell his sons to do at night at the river? Who did this task?

3) Knowing Baba Buddha Jee's thoughts what did Guru Jee ask him? Who obeyed Guru Jee's words in the end?

4) When Guru Jee asked the Sikhts to eat the dead body what did the Sikhs do? What did Sri Lehna Jee see when he was about to eat it?

Chapter 23
Sri Guru Nanak Dev Jee goes to Sachkand

Like any other day, Kirtan was taking place in the Diwan (communal congregation) at Kartarpur. Some time had passed with Guru Jee sitting there and They now said, "We are going to Sachkand today," (Sachkand is the highest spiritual realm). Guru Jee said to Bhai Sadharn Jee, "Bring Sri Chand and Lakhmi Das here."

Bhai Sadharn Jee went to bring Guru Jee's sons and said to them, "Guru Jee is leaving for Sachkand. He has called for you."

They replied, "How have They got ready to leave so quickly?"

After saying this, they refused to go with Bhai Sadharn Jee.

When Guru Jee's wife, Mata Sulakhni Jee, learnt that her Guru and husband is ready to leave earth, she was upset that her sons had been disobedient. She was overcome with emotions and came to Guru Jee. Guru Jee said to her, "You are of good fortune. Speak about whatever you like then you cannot say after that you didn't have this final opportunity."

Mata Jee said in submission, "Get all the congregation together and give everyone your darshan before leaving. For this reason, stay for one more day."

Guru Jee said, "You have spoken correctly. We will leave in two days' time now."

Hearing this, the Sikhs were pleased. From that day, Guru Jee got many different dishes made in the Langar and fed them to the Sikhs. Hearing of Guru Jee's impending departure, congregations of Sikhs came from afar. Kartarpur became very crowded. Everyone was crying, knowing of Guru Jee's imminent departure. Mata Sulakhni Jee remained by Guru Jee's side obediently. Everyone was depressed. Seeing this state of the Sikhs, Guru Jee said, "All our bodies will perish and we depart from them. Those people who become one with the Shabad/Gurbani, they never depart (as they are liberated). Those who want to meet Us should meditate upon Gurbani. Those who imbue Naam in their minds, They are never separated. The whole world is perishable." In this way, Guru Jee taught the Sikhs and eased their minds, giving them some solace and peace.

The day dawned for Guru Jee's departure. Guru Jee came out of the Dharamsala. Guru Jee got a spread laid out to sit upon and got a tent constructed. Mata Sulakhni Jee now made an appeal to Guru Jee, "Now, call your sons or afterwards they will live in regret. It is important they are here with you now."

Hearing this, Guru Jee dispatched a Sikh to fetch his sons. The Sikh went and said to Guru Jee's sons, "Guru Jee is about to merge His body back into God. Come and have Their darshan and have your final words with Them."

The sons replied, "They said they were going to merge three days ago, in the same way they will merge today." Saying this, they refused to go to Guru Jee. The Sikh returned and informed Guru Jee of this and Guru Jee remained silent.

Guru Jee said to everyone, "All leave this tent and meditate on God's true name." The Sikhs left the tent and Guru Jee put a white sheet over Themselves. Commotion broke out between the Sikhs that Guru Jee has departed for Sachkand. Everyone started to cry. Hearing the wails, Baba Sri Chand and Baba Lakhmi Das came and humbly made a plea to Guru Jee, "All powerful father, we didn't realise you would actually merge back with God without having final words with us. Please give us darshan for two more gharia (approximately forty eight minutes).” Acknowledging this, Guru Jee got up and said, “If you had asked for Me to live longer then I would have agreed but you only asked for two gharia. Whatever God wills only that occurs. Now, tell me whatever is on your minds.”

Baba Sri Chand clasped his hands and said, “Sons inherit their father’s legacy. You have given Lehna the Guruship, and not given us anything. What you have done is wrong. We are your sons - keep the honour of your name (meaning family lineage).”

Guru Jee replied, “Receiving and giving is in the hands of the creator   God.”

The sons replied, “We have no power in front of you.”

Guru Jee now replied, “You will have ridhia sidhia (spiritual powers and the ability to do miracles). You will lack no worldly goods. Sikhs will worship you as the people of the world even worship the dogs of Gurus and Saints. You are my sons. Why would they not believe in you? But the praise of Gurbani and being one with it - is Sri Angad’s. Do not be in anguish over this.”

The two Gharia had transpired in this time so everyone was told to leave the tent again. Guru Jee put the sheet over Themselves and went with Their body to Sachkand. While Guru Jee was travelling to Sachkand on their celestial vehicle, the angels showered Guru Jee with flowers and bellowed out praise and celebrated. Guru Jee went to Sachkand.

While back at Kartarpur, an extraordinary argument broke out over the conduct of the funeral. The Hindus argued that they wanted to cremate the body but the Muslims wanted to bury it. Both sides argued about this. Baba Buddha Jee, and

107

other wise Sikhs, said, "Do not argue – let us have Guru Jee's advice."

When they went inside, they found no body under the sheet. The two opposing sides took the sheet and halved it, each getting a half of the sheet. The Muslims made a raised grave with the sheet in it and the Hindus built a platform where they did the cremation of the sheet. Both communities started worshipping each site reverently – the grave and place of cremation.

Guru Jee did not like either of these practices. The River Ravi then flooded the site, destroying both sites.

On 7th September 1539 CE, Guru Jee went to Sachkand. Guru Jee spent sixty nine years, ten months and eighteen days on earth. Today, Kartarpur Gurdwara stands where this all occurred in Pakistan.

Revision Questions Chapter 23

1) When Bhai Sadharn went to fetch Guru Jee's sons what did they say?

2) What did Mata Sulakhni Jee ask Guru Jee to do when they said they are going to depart?

3) After Guru Jee passed, what did Guru Jee's sons ask Guru Jee to do?

4) When Guru Jee left for Sachkand what argument broke out?

Glossary

Amrit   Immortal nectar

Amrit Vela   The last three hours before dawn, which is especially tranquil and best for meditation

Ang   Limb. Used to denote page numbers when referring to Sri Guru Granth Sahib Jee – the current eternal Guru of the Sikhs, which is an anthology of prayers. The Sikhs believe Sri Guru Granth Sahib Jee to be a living embodiment of the Gurus hence why the word 'ang' is used.

Antarjami   Knower of hearts – someone who knows your thoughts

Ardas   Supplication prayer, conducted standing up, usually after prayers and/or during specific points in different ceremonies

Atma   Soul

Atma-Gian   Wisdom of the soul

Avatar   An incarnation of a higher being or God

Baba   Respected elder. Can also refer to a paternal grandfather.

Bairaag   Detachment from the world

Bazaar	Shopping precinct
Bhagat	Devotee
Bhagti	Devotional practices
Bhandara	A feast. Usually held to feed saints.
Brahm Bhoj	A ceremonial feast in which 'Brahmins' are fed first
Brahma	Angel of creation
Brahmin	Hindu priestly caste
Charan Pahul	Initiation ceremony of Sikhi. The initiate drank water that has been blessed by the touching of the feet of the Guru. This has been now replaced by Khande dee Pahul, water transformed into immortal nectar via stirring a double-edged sword in a cauldron by five blessed Sikhs.
Chownka	A sacred square that is purified. Used in Hindu practices.
Devte	Angels
Darshan place	Blessed sight of a special person or
Darvesh	Sufi Saints who are mostly renunciates
Dharamsala	Place of worship and congregation, where free food and accommodation would be given to travellers

Diwan	Court or the holding of a congregation
Gurbani	Words of the Guru – Sikh Scripture
Gurmantar	A word that a Guru imparts to his disciple in inducting them. It is a word that must be meditated upon at all times.
Guru	Enlightener – someone who brings you the light of wisdom and takes you away from ignorance
Ishnaan	Bathing. Sikhs meditate whilst bathing to cleanse externally and internally.
Jee	A suffix added to denote respect
Jhamdhoot	Death's angels/messengers that reside in the afterlife, they come to collect the person who has died to take them to their next destination. These jhamdhoot can be both demonic and saintly, depending on your level of sin or goodness.
Jug	Aeon, there are four of these. Kaljug the age of sin being the present one.
Kaal	Time or death
Kaljug	Current era of sin

Karah Parshad A blessed sweet food, that is distributed at Gurdwaras, made of ghee, water, sugar and flour.

Khatri   Warrior caste

Khraava   A wooden sandal, a very old design of
footwear

Kirtan   Devotional singing of hymns, in Sikhi this is singing Gurbani (words of the Guru's, scriptures)

Langar   Free blessed food, usually consisting of a meal, served to anyone at most Gurdwaras – Sikh places of worship.

Maharaj   Great king. Used as term of reverence too.

Marasi   Low caste, usually minstrels by trade
and/or attendants

Mullah   A Muslim priest

Naam   The name of God

Nirgun Upasna
                Praying to God in a formless manner.

Panja   Refers to a hand, panj means five, panja means hand with five fingers

Panja Sahib   A Gurdwara where Sri Guru Nanak Dev Jee's handprint is permanently visible in a rock

Pandit	A religious scholar, priest and in the Hindu faith Brahmins
Parkarma	Circumambulation
Rakash	A demon, the opposite of an Angel
Sachkand	The highest spiritual realm, literally translates to 'realm of truth'
Sahib	Means master, also used as a suffix when addressing someone respectfully
Sargun Upasna	Praying to God in the creation
Satjug	Aeon of truth.
Satsang	True congregation where only God is meditated upon and/or discussed
Seva	Voluntary devotional service
Shabad	A verse from Sikh Scripture
Shau	Lord/God
Shiva	Angel of destruction
Shoodar	Low caste
Sikh	A disciple/follower of the Sikh Gurus
Sikhi	Teachings of the Sikh Gurus
Simran	Meditation

Sohagan	Happy bride/wife
Sri	Supreme, usually used as a prefix to add respect
Sukh	Pleasure but has a very wide purview to include things which illicit this pleasure such as peace, tranquillity and so forth
Sukhi	To be in a state of pleasure or happiness.
Tap	Penance, stringent meditations
Tapa	A meditative person or someone who has done hard penances and/or meditation or studies
Vishnu	Angel of sustenance
Yag	A Hindu sacrificial ceremony

Answers to all revision questions

Chapter 1 Answers

1. Bhai Lalo lived in Eminabad, he was a very devout carpenter. Guru Jee said he was very saintly.
2. Bhai Mardana said the food tasted like Amrit. Bhai Lalo said, "Greatness is all yours, as yours are great. You look at the heart-felt devotion and don't judge the food that is cooked. You have abolished the anguish of many lives of mine and have made all my efforts fruitful. You are forever merciful to your slaves (servants)."
3. "That is the Marasi of the one who is treading the wrong path."
4. To go home to Talvandi

Chapter 2 Answers

1. Malik Bhago was a minister of the Governor of Eminabad. He conducted the Bhram Bhoj to get more popular in the area.
2. Blood came out of Malik Bhago's chapatti and milk came out of Bhai Lalo's.
3. Guru Jee said, "It is from this money of suffering that you have organised this Brahm Bhoj. Eating this food destroys your good actions. Those who do not know this are happily drinking this blood of sin in the food. They are polluting their own minds by eating this food."
4. Guru Jee said, "Eating from Bhai Lalo's house is a daily Brahm Bhoj which is why I eat at his house. He makes food from an honest living."

Chapter 3 Answers

1. Guru Jee told him to eat a poisonous fruit called crown plant
2. Bhai Mardana ate the fruit he had hidden earlier. He was cured by eating some more of this fruit which was given to him from Guru Jee's blessed hands

Chapter 4 Answers

1. Kamru Desh is in modern day Assam and is called Kamru region
2. Bhai Mardana was transformed into a sheep through a spell of the evil women
3. Guru Jee went and stood outside the house where Bhai Mardana was tied. The women were very happy upon seeing Guru Jee. Two women came forward with strings in their hands and they were reading incantations (spells) as they walked forward. One of them was about to put a string over Bhai Bala's head but she immediately became a sheep. The second women came forward to put the string over Guru Jee but she immediately became a female dog (bitch). The other women quickly ran indoors.
   The womens husbands arrived and they begged for forgiveness and they all agreed to give up their sinful ways and become Sikhs.
4. Guru Jee said, "Take on our teachings of Sikhi and build a Dharamsala (a place of worship and sanctuary) where you will conduct daily congregations (satsang) in the morning and evening. Here, you should serve Sikhs and Saints which will be for your betterment. At death the death's angels will not then make you suffer. Give up your lives of sin and earn an honest living."

Chapter 5 Answers

1. Kauda was liberated in a jungle. There is Gurdwara there today.
2. Bhai Mardana was 11 hours if Guru Jee walked to him
3. Guru Jee cooled the oil cauldron down with their powers and to save Bhai Mardana. Kauda was shocked when the oil cooled down and he got out his mirror and Guru Jee reflected as a human being and Kauda fell at Guru Jee's feet.
4. Kauda described how he disrespected his Guru in a previous life and was cursed to be a demon. He was told he would be redeemed by God's Avatar (reincarnation) who would save him from his demonic form.
5. Kauda was told only the Avatar would reflect in this mirror as a human being, all others would portray previous lifeforms they had been through and not show as a human.

Chapter 6 Answers

1. To dispel his greed and help the people who lived there
2. He had robbed the population of its wealth. His brother Haru accumulated a lot of wealth and put it in 40 treasure chests but through tyranny Karu has increased this to 45 treasure chests.
3. "Announce in the whole country that whoever gives 1 rupee they will be married to my daughter."
4. He asked for 1 Rupee, his mother told him to get it from the mouth of his dead father, from within his grave

5. Karu then got all the 1 Rupees removed from all graves
6. They were collecting shards of pottery
7. Nasihatnama

Chapter 7 Answers

1. They were scared of a fire breaking out which would burn the whole village. This used to happen every six months. The time for the fire was in a few days.
2. Guru Jee said, "If you become our Sikhs then your homes will not burn down. Meditate on God's True Name, abolish fear from your hearts. Dwell in your homes with peace."
3. He said "You stayed here and no longer feared me. I will not spare you now and will eat you."
4. Seeing the people tremble in fear Guru Jee looked at the demon in anger. The demon immediately fainted. His head fell towards the feet of Guru Jee and Guru Jee felt mercy for him. Guru Jee put his foot on to the head of the demon. The demon then came about from being unconscious.
5. Guru Jee said to the demon, "Build a Dharamsala (place of workshop) in this village, all the village should congregate there to meditate and sing God's praises. All your sins will thus be abolished. Bring water by carrying it on your head (in pitchers) for the congregation and sing God's praises. Then you will get liberated."

Chapter 8 Answers

1. Guru Jee said, "Climb this hillock. At the peak a powerful Muslim saint resides there called Vali Kandahari. He has gathered water from waterfalls and made a man-made lake. Go and ask him for drinking water."

2. He said, "If he is a miracle worker, then why can he not summon water to himself where he is seated? It is right, to give the thirsty, water, but after hearing your words, I will not give you water." He was jealous and burnt in anger hearing Guru Jee's praise.
3. All the water that the Peer had on the hilltop was now transferred below, to where Guru Jee was (at the bottom/base of the hill)
4. He rolled the rock down the hill to stop the water coming out of the spring that Guru Jee had created. Guru Jee stopped the rock wth His hand, creating a handprint in the rock (panja)
5. Vali Kandahari was given water from rainfall which always replenishes his man-made lake – it never runs out.

Chapter 9 Answers

1. In Kabul, Afghanistan
2. To destroy the anger of the Mullah, Guru Jee sat on top of the Mosque and made the whole Mosque fly around the city of Kabul
3. Guru Jee made the mosque now face the West as opposed to the North
4. They asked for Guru Jee's shoes (kharaava)
5. Muslims believe the mosque should face the North so they tried to make it do this again as it was now facing the West. After changing the direction of the mosque to the North, during the night it shifted again to now face the West again.

Chapter 10 Answers

1. Bhai Bala was made a newly wedded bride of 16 years old and Guru Jee was dressed as the husband of this bride.

2. They told the thief to steal all Guru Jee's possessions and to share them in the morning

3. Guru Jee asked them to ensure that they cremate them. Guru Jee told them to get fire with which they could light their pyre with.

4. They saw a man been beaten by death's angels and being dragged to his funeral pyre. They then saw the same man being carried on a carriage with honour by the same death's angels. They then learnt that this man's sins were all abolished by just having the sight (darshan) of Guru Jee.

5. Guru Jee said, "Give up the murder of others and start farming for a living. All the money and possessions gained from the money of sinful actions - give it all to others." Earn an honest living with your own hands. Out of your earnings do good and share with others. Make a Dharamsala (place of worship) in your village, feed the needy and Saints. Forever meditate upon God, which will eradicate all your sins. Before dawn (Amrit Vela) rise and meditate. During the day do your work. In the evenings congregate in the Dharmsala to meditate on God. Do these things and your lives will become worthwhile."

Chapter 11 Answers

1. He used to say God used to come to meet him on the second night after the full moon

2. Shau-Sohagan replied he only meets God on that day of the festival and no other, so he did not meet Guru Jee in person and refused them entry into his room

3. Violence and looting broke out. People got injured and some died too.

4. Shau-Sohagan was caught sleeping with a woman and was thrown out for being a fake saint. People looted all his belongings too.

5. Guru Jee cured a man with disabilities and told the man to tell everyone that Shau-Sohagan had cured him. Guru Jee then put Shau-Sohagan on the right path of being honest and devout and reinstalled his fame and respect. Guru Jee told him to openly meet people and not hide in his room.

Chapter 12 Answers

1. The residents of Kanganpur were very egotistical and sinful, they behaved badly with all that they met. They offered no food or drink to Guru Jee and threw stones at them to make them leave.

2. The people of Manakdeke were of a very good nature, they would serve guests who came to their village and helped everyone as much as they could. They served Guru Jee with great passion.

3. Guru Jee wanted the sinful villagers to stay where they were so they do not spread their bad habits. Guru Jee wanted the good villagers to disperse so they could spread their good ways with others.

Chapter 13 Answers

1. Kaval Nain ruled Swaranpur and had 17 other kingdoms aligned to him

2. Dharam Singh told Bhai Mardana all the food was free, Bhai Mardana said he would only eat the food after Dharam Singh passed it to him with his own hands

3. Guru Jee said, "No one sins here. There is a big Dharamsala (place of worship) here. Sin has left the whole nation. The residents here are content and

honest, living sinless lives. They all love doing good actions."

4. Guru Jee refused the food as he said the king was at fault and wouldn't eat from his kingdom

5. Guru Jee told him about his previous life when he served King Janak and how he was blessed with a boon to become the future king that he was and that Guru Jee would also liberate him.

Chapter 14 Answers

1. Saudi Arabia

2. 3 readers. "There are three ways to read a book. Like eating a bone, eating meat and eating seeds. To read a book and then enter needless debates about its contents, is like trying to eat a bone. To read a book and then become respected and get others to serve you is like eating meat. Those who read it then meditate on God's name, those who see God in all and pray for the betterment of all, those readers are like those eating seeds."

3. He saw a black stone

4. Jeevan kicked Guru Jee and tried to move their feet away from the direction of the Kaaba but the Kaaba moved to wherever Guru Jee's feet were pointing.

5. He threw the Shiva-ling out of his kingdom then a lot of things and buildings burnt down in his kingdom.

6. Shiva Jee told him to build a temple and place the Shiva-ling inside and that anyone who sees the Shiva-ling will go blind, thus people should only go near it whilst being blindfolded.

Chapter 15 Answers

1. Bhai Mardana said, "Oh my beloved with your blessings we have travelled thousands of miles quickly

– for that reason, I do not see it as being far away. You are the form of God who has come to liberate people on earth in Kaljug (present era of sin)."

2. Guru Jee spoke a Shabad and the Prophet Mohammad's tomb came forward and lowered itself to Guru Jee's feet.

3. Guru Jee said, "Remember your death at all times. Relinquish sin and difference in people, see God in all. Medit

4. ate on God's name. You will then not enter hells. Give up hypocrisy or outwardly appearances, commit yourselves to true devotion to God's name, by doing this you will experience pleasure in everything you do."

5. Guru Jee had a stick and they hit it with great force into the wall of the Kaaba and water now started flowing from the hole that was created.

Chapter 16 Answers

1. People were throwing water towards the sun in the hope that it reaches and helps their ancestors. Guru Jee threw water in the opposite direction towards his fields.

2. Guru Jee said if my water is falling back into the river and cannot reach my fields then how can your water reach your anscetors

3. That they were false and all engrossed in worldly affairs, even if they were outwardly using rosaries. Guru Jee described the state and location of their minds when using the rosaries.

4. Guru Jee said the square is polluted by the entry of the Brahmins/Pandits as they sin so much

Corrupt intellect is the minstrel woman (mirasi caste); cruelty is the female butcher; slander of others in one's heart is the cleaning-woman (choori) and extreme anger and violence is the

outcast-woman (chandalani). What good are the ceremonial lines drawn around your kitchen, when these four women of sin are seated there with you? (91 Ang)

The Pandits asked, "How can the square become purified now, then?" Guru Jee then uttered these lines continuing this Shabad,

"Make truth your self-discipline, make good deeds the lines you draw; make chanting God's name your cleansing bath. O Nanak, those who do not walk in the ways of sin, shall be exalted in the world hereafter. (91 Ang)

5. The River Ganga said, "Oh God, I cannot carry the burden of sins in Kaljug. Please bless me with a solution with which I can be at peace and in bliss (sukhi) always. You have taken on a human body to help others."

   Guru Jee said to the River Ganga, "In the mornings and in the evenings think of God's believers. When they put their blessed feet in your water all the sins you are burdened with, will be destroyed.'

   Guru Jee also said 'This tray of jewels is of no use to us. Use it to feed Saints that are dedicated to God (to do a Bhandara – a feast for Saints)."

Chapter 17 Answers

1. He was tricked into the home of a woman, she put a thread around him which had a spell on it and he was made a sheep
2. Guru Jee got the water pitcher stuck on her head

3. She said 'God is the wonderful enlightener' as instructed by Guru Jee and then removed the water pitcher from her head.

4. Guru Jee advised them, "Meditate on the wonderous enlightener God at all times, God will destroy all anguish from your lives. Whoever comes here, do not use spells on them. Instead serve any visitors as guests." Guru Jee also got them to build a Dharamsala and told them to do daily Sadh Sangat.

Chapter 18 Answers

1. Guru Jee arrived there after descending down from other mountains and after speaking to the Yogis

2. He asked who authored the Shabad

3. Guru Jee described five types of listener, Guru Jee said "There are 5 types of listeners. One who understands the Raag (musical tune), secondly those who understand the notes, thirdly those who understand the beat, fourthly those who listen to music and fifthly those who understand the hymn – who are supreme.

4. Kagh Bhasund said, "My age is beyond example or counting. When 100 ages (jugs) pass, it is one night of Brahma and a further 100 years (jug) pass for a day of his. I have seen many Brahmas die, who each die after 100 years. I have seen destruction many times of the whole world and then a new Brahma starts to create the world again."

5. He was disobedient and disrespectful. With his first Guru, Manchain he opposed devotion to Vishnu. Then, with Lomas Rikhi he repeatedly went against his advice to do Nirgun Upasana

6. Lomas Rikhi cursed him due to his argumentative nature and disobedience.

Chapter 19 Answers

1. From the Sumer mountain Guru Jee went on to meet Bhagat Prehlad, Datta Dhre and others, and then arrived at Dhrus planet.
2. "If you desire the throne, then die and be reborn to me."
3. She said that she is in a less powerful position than the step-mother as she has not done enough devotion to God and she taught Dhru that through meditation he can overcome all obstacles.
4. Dhru started doing very difficult penance, after every three days he would eat some fruits from the jungle. He passed the first month like this. In the second month he started eating only grass. In the third month he ate dry leaves and drank water only. In the fourth month he ate every 12 days. In the fifth month he survived only an on air and stood on one foot whilst meditating.
5. They killed his brother. His grandfather Manu instructed him to stop the war against them as Dhru had killed many of them yet only one brother of his had been killed.
6. 36,000 years. At death on earth he was given the North star as his own planet to rule over.

Chapter 20 Answers

1. Sajjan was dressed like a Saint but was a thief who would rob and murder guests.
2. Sajjan welcomed Shehzada in and offered him food. Shehzada was then beaten and tied up, all his belongings were robbed off him
3. Maharaj told him to meditate on God at all times and to give out all his wealth to the poor.
4. Sajjan was told to make Shehzada his Guru

Chapter 21 Answers

1. Name of original village was Matte Dee Sarai. Fathers name was Phiru Mal and mother was Deya Kaur (Sabhrayee) Jee.
2. It is in Kangra
3. Bhai Jodha Jee
4. Guru Jee said, "Those who are going to take (meaning Lehna) they come seated upon a mare. Those who are going to give, they come by walking."
5. Guru Jee said, "This pile of grass that he carried upon his head, is giving him the crown of ruling the whole world. What you see as mud is us spraying saffron upon him." This meant that through this seva they would become the next Guru.

Chapter 22 Answers

1. Seeing the people hungry Guru Jee said to his eldest son Baba Sri Chand "That tree which is there, go and shake it. Then a multitude of foods, desserts and dishes will fall from it, the people who are hungry can then eat." Both sons refused to do this and Sri Lehna did it when asked by Guru Jee
2. One night, Guru Jee said to his eldest son Baba Sri Chand Jee, "Son, go and wash and dry this sheet at the river." He refused to do this as did Baba Lakhmi Das. Sri Lehna did this at the first asking.
3. So, at night Guru Jee said, "Buddha, go out and have a look at how much nightfall is remaining. Is it time to do Ishnaan or not?"
   Baba Buddha Jee went out and looked and said, "Half the night is left."
   Guru Jee said "No there is not that much left of it, only three hours remain."

Baba Buddha Jee repeatedly disagreed with Guru Jee upon the amount of nightfall left but Sri Lehna humbly accepted Guru Jee's assessment after disagreeing once.

4. The Sikhs all left and hid. He saw karah parshad there.

Chapter 23 Answers

1. They replied, "How have they got ready to leave so quickly?" After saying this they refused to go with Bhai Sadharn Jee.

2. She asked Guru Jee to stay for one more day, so more Sikhs could have their darshan. Guru Jee said they would stay two more days

3. Hearing the wails Baba Sri Chand and Baba Lakhmi Das came and humbly made a plea to Guru Jee, "All powerful father, we didn't realise you would actually merge back with God, without having final words with us, for this reason please give us darshan for 2 more Gharia (approximately 48 mins)." Guru Jee agreed and have a conversation with them.

4. The Hindus and Muslims argued about the funeral. They found no body and each did the funeral rites according to their faiths with the sheet that was left. Muslims made a tomb and the Hindus cremated the sheet.

Printed in Great Britain
by Amazon